Philip

The missing God who is not missed
CHRISTIAN BELIEF IN A SECULAR SOCIETY

the columba press

First published in 2003 by
the columba press
55A Spruce Avenue, Stillorgan Industrial Park,
Blackrock, Co Dublin

Cover by Bill Bolger
Origination by The Columba Press
Printed in Ireland by ColourBooks Ltd, Dublin

ISBN 1 85607 380 7

Contents

Introduction

If the old forms of atheism and agnosticism are now out of date, it is clear that one cannot yet proclaim the reflourishing of theism. What more truly characterises the present moment is that the question of God remains irrelevant, or even non-existent for the great majority of people. 'God is missing but not missed.' That is a genuinely new situation which never existed before in the world. (Josep Vives SJ)

We live a technological, scientific age where people tend to accept as real only what they can see, experience for themselves or prove scientifically. Anything else is seen as mere conjecture. Since we cannot see God or prove God's existence with the tools of science, more and more of us assume that God's existence is but one theory among many. While not excluding faith and all reference to God, there is a slow but inexorable move towards agnosticism.

Modern culture is deeply stamped by the natural and human sciences where psychology is constantly discovering new, almost immeasurable depths in the human psyche, and quantum theory is forcing us to look at the world in unimaginably new ways. But does science have the last word about God's existence? If there is no God there is, of course, no argument or intellectual exercise that can create one. On the other hand, no successful scientific explanations, or seeming inconsistencies between science and belief, can cause God *not* to exist. If God does exist, only freely exercised faith, such as validates the sort of faith and trust that can exist between human beings, can validate

but God is not a person....

faith in God and unite people to the One whose nature they reflect, even if only as 'in a glass darkly'.

What we should accept from science and from religion is not always as clear-cut or as stark as has often been depicted. While scientists may well doubt the story of Jonah being swallowed by a large fish, to take but one example, they, like many fundamentalists, often fail to realise that the story of Jonah is simply a *parable* about the mercy of God. On the other hand, the belief that Jesus rose from the dead, which is a central tenet of Christianity, does seem to conflict with the insistence by biologists that such a thing is impossible. Yet, even here, as we shall see later, the conflict between science and religion is not as stark as it might appear.

'To dismiss belief in God summarily is to pass premature and unwarranted judgment on the sanity, honesty, and intelligence of a vast number of our fellow human beings who claim to have such experiential evidence, many of them the same persons we do trust implicitly when it comes to other matters. It ill becomes any of us to take the attitude that all evidence for God is false evidence, beneath consideration, simply by virtue of its being evidence for God, or even by virtue of its being outside the purview of science. Such attitudes are taken, sometimes in the name of science, but in truth this sort of attitude *is* intellectual dishonesty. Our most reputable scientists, whatever sins of arrogance they may occasionally commit, do not really declare that what they don't know isn't knowledge or that what they haven't experienced isn't experience.'[1]

Another major influence that can lead us towards agnosticism is the dominant economic system that, consciously or unconsciously, affects the way most of us think and act – capitalism. The most extreme expression of the capitalist ethic may be that ascribed to Margaret Thatcher: the legitimate pursuit of self-interest in a competitive environment in which market forces operate freely and in which profit is the driving mechanism! In the capitalist system the 'market' is the regulator of all economic activity and deeply influences social relationships. The Commodity Market determines the conditions under which commodities are exchanged. Cornflakes, for example, have no economic, no exchange value of themselves unless people wish to buy them. So, since the system needs people who consume more and more, conscious efforts are made by producers to standardise peoples' tastes through advertising so that what they buy can be influenced and even anticipated.

The Labour Market, on the other hand, regulates the acquisition and sale of human labour. Human energy and skills are often treated as commodities and are valued only in so far as they can be bought and sold. Those who have few skills or are disadvantaged in some way tend to find themselves pushed to the margins of society. Those who own capital buy human labour and put it to work as a profitable investment. Those who have to sell their labour must sell it to the owner of capital under existing market conditions unless they wish to starve. In such a system people easily become 'cogs' in the economic machine, useful until they become 'surplus to requirements' and are then simply made 'redundant'.

a bit OTT. Third World maybe...

With the ever-increasing centralisation and concentration of capital, large corporations grow in size, continuously squeezing out the smaller ones. Thousands of stockholders 'own' the enterprise and employ a well paid managerial bureaucracy to manage it. But bureaucrats too can become 'cogs' in the economic enterprise and can just as easily become 'surplus to requirements'!

off the point a bit

Buying and selling infiltrate every aspect of our lives and behaviour, so we can easily come to believe that what we own, or the skills we have to offer the market, are what determine our worth as human beings. 'Will I sell?' 'Will they buy me?' are not simply questions that teenagers ask!

This is why so many elderly, retired people succumb to the ✓
feeling of being worthless and discarded once their marketability days are over.

Productivity, marketability and consumption are not, of
course, evils in themselves and can be beneficial to human
development provided that the well-being of customers,
suppliers, employees and the local community are all
taken into account. But when the relation of people to production is reversed; when the products produced or consumed are seen as more important than human well-being
or when we value ourselves solely in terms of external crit-
eria, then the possession of 'things' can begin to rule or
even ruin our lives. 'Man cannot relinquish himself or the
place in the visible world that belongs to him; he cannot
become the slave of things, the slave of economic systems,
the slave of production, the slave of his own products.' [2]

'Another way of putting this problem is to suggest
what kinds of behaviour are "not good news for business".
Let us suppose that you are a married person with children. If you are relatively happy with your life, if you enjoy
spending time with your children, playing with them and
talking with them; if you like nature, if you enjoy sitting in
your yard or on your front doorsteps, if your sexual life is
relatively happy, if you have a peaceful sense of who you
are and are stabilised in your relationships, if you like to
pray in solitude, if you just like talking to people, visiting
them, spending time in conversation with them, if you
enjoy living simply, if you sense no need to compete with
your friends or neighbours – *what good are you economically*
in terms of our system? You haven't spent a nickel yet.   Kavanaugh

'However if you are unhappy and distressed, if you are ✓
living in anxiety and confusion, if you are unsure of your-
self and your relationships, if you find no happiness in
your family or sex life, if you can't bear being alone or living simply – you will crave much. You will want more.
You will have the behaviours most suitable to a social system
that is based upon continual economic growth.'[3]

Advertising, the 'life-blood' of the capitalist system, is quite ready to exploit such anxiety and confusion and even create false needs in order get us to buy more. The fear of solitude, of intimacy, the tendency of people to value themselves in terms of what others, particularly the rich and famous do, think or possess, the quantifiable inability of many people to form enduring relationships, are always nudging us into possessing and accumulating more and more to fill up the vacuum in our lives. The consumerist culture throws thousands of images at us, creating envy among the poor and fostering the notion that a happy life is defined by material possessions where the superficial becomes desirable, the desirable becomes necessary and the necessary becomes essential! Since possessions alone, however, can never fill the 'hungers of the heart', or answer the need for committed mutual love or provide meaning to life, escapism and even hedonism are offered as 'buyable' substitutes.

Economic factors also tend to determine where people live and work. In the past they lived in more or less homogeneous groups. There was great solidarity between people in the countryside, in villages and even in towns and Christian faith was a living reality for most people. Contemporary society has witnessed the disintegration of such communities. More and more people are drawn to the large urban areas seeking work or social and economic advantage. There they find a widely differing mix of philosophies and a veritable 'supermarket' of values disseminated by the media beyond the influence of religious institutions. They also find a great disparity between rich and poor. Given that situation, human solidarity quickly breaks down and is often replaced by a competitive, aggressive individualism and consumerism.

As the traditional values that bound older communities together disintegrate, there is a gradual atomisation of society: a loss of a sense of identity with and responsibility for the larger political and social issues facing society. Allied to this is a widespread feeling of being impotent before the forces that govern society: governments, corporate institutions and churches are widely regarded with suspicion or apathy. Hence people are less willing to see themselves as parts of a wider society to which they owe responsibility and withdraw into the narrow world of personal relationships with family and friends. If religion does play a part in peoples' lives, it tends to be seen as something very personal and private – a point of view that is essentially at odds with the Christian gospel.

It is no accident then that God is often 'missing but not missed' and questions about God, who seems to be 'above and beyond' the strains and stresses of the market place, seem irrelevant to many people. Today's religious vacuum is part of a larger unease and uncertainty about values, about institutions, about the possibility of finding livable meanings to life. So what Christians are experiencing today is quite different from anything that went on in the past and has distinctive features that make it not only new but unique. The dominance of the capitalist-ethic and the breakdown in social cohesion, allied to the 'privatising' of religion, have all combined to make Christian faith seem 'irrelevant', especially to the poor and the marginalised. Many people today put their 'faith' in science, believing that it will eventually make religion redundant by giving us a complete understanding of not only 'how' the universe came into existence but also the 'why' of its existence. Perhaps it is worth noting the words of Stephen Hawking: 'I think I may find out "how" but I am not optimistic about finding out "why". If I knew that, I would know everything important.'

The church has inevitably been affected by the 'faith' that people place in science and the capitalist ethic, as well as by the disintegration of traditional communities and value systems. There has been a huge decline in church attendance especially among the poor and among middle-class young people, a dramatic falloff in religious vocations, and a loss of moral credibility owing to the large-scale rejection of the church's teaching about contraception. The church is also suffering from the tragic involvement of some of its priests in child sexual abuse and other forms of abuse that have taken place in religious institutions. Such abuses have blighted the lives of many victims and dented the morale of priests worldwide, contributing as they do to a serious breakdown of trust between priests and people.

The rigid authoritarianism of the past is no longer accepted unquestioningly, while participation, especially by the poor and by women, in the decision making process of the church, in the spirit of Vatican II, was, and still is, largely ignored. Nor have the divisions within and between the Christian churches helped the situation.

The church's former appeal leaned heavily on a certain externalism expressed in popular devotions, especially Marian devotions. As the liturgical reforms of Vatican II began to take hold, many of these devotions simply lapsed. Quoting the parable of the Sower, one could say that, in recent decades, God's Word 'sprang up on rocky ground where it withered for lack of roots. For others the seed fell among thorns and was choked because worldly anxiety, the lure of riches and the craving for other things intruded and choked the Word.'[4]

Churchmen have tended to attribute the decline in religious faith and practice simply to a growing secularism, to ignorance, indifference, or rebellion against the church, and it is true that these have all been factors in recent church history. But church leaders must also bear some responsibility for the fact that 'God is missing but not missed'.

In such an ocean of uncertainties many age-old questions about Christian faith still cry out for answers. How can we reconcile the existence of God with all the suffering

in the world? Is the God of the Bible nothing but a vengeful God? Who is Jesus? Was he just a good man or was he
truly divine? Did he rise from the dead? What do we mean
when we say that Jesus is the saviour of the world and is
he the only saviour? Whatever happened to hell? Can we
still believe in miracles? Why have so many young people
and the poor given up on the church and sacramental
practice? Are priests no more than lumbering dinosaurs?

Let me make one final point of introduction. I use male
pronouns in speaking of God not because I believe that
God is male, which is clearly as ridiculous as suggesting
that God is female. I simply follow Jesus' way of speaking
about God with no desire to adopt patriarchal attitudes!

1. God irrelevant
2. Consumer Capitalism

} MB ∃ a link but
its not as
definitive as
PF says

Is God Unfair?

how related to (1) + (2)?

CHAPTER 1

Is God Unfair?

But you have to think he exists before you can ask whether or not he's unfair.

How can we believe in God when there are such terrible sufferings in the world: when someone we love is taken away in death or becomes incurably ill; when we see children suffering from serious mental or physical disorders; when we stand at the coffin of a seventeen year old friend or watch the slow death of ageing parents; when we see starvation in Africa or the old dying of hypothermia on the streets of Dublin; how can all this fit into God's scheme of things? Why does God not prevent such suffering? Either God cannot and so God is not all-powerful, or God will not and so can hardly be called good. Is God simply disinterested and above all human suffering while we struggle and suffer here on earth? Is God indifferent or impotent? Is God nothing more than a cruel despot?

God's seeming unfairness can haunt us as we struggle to reconcile a God of love and the depths of human suffering. It may be impossible to reconcile the immensity of human suffering with the mystery of a loving God in a way that fully satisfies the human heart. However, there may be ways of thinking about the problem that can at least give us some insight and provide renewed strength and hope. To begin, we need to remind ourselves that we live in an evolving world.

The theory of evolution seeks to explain the origins of the different species on earth, their modifications and sometimes their extinction. It accounts for the variability, adaptation, and distribution of living organisms that take place over millions of years. Evolution is determined by

"Sometimes" is wrong. it's over-and-over again

the 'laws' of nature, which govern how things come to be, change and adapt. Without such laws the universe would simply not exist – *nor would we.*

Millions of years ago, scientists tell us, the universe erupted spontaneously into existence – out of nothing; an event popularly termed the Big Bang. The Big Bang is the earliest event in the history of the universe accessible to science – that singular moment in which cosmic matter appears to have exploded from a point of infinite compression. Space and time made their appearance with the Big Bang and the process of evolution began.

Some scientists believe that the universe continues to expand indefinitely. For others, however, evolution is moving, imperceptibly but inexorably, from the Big Bang towards the Big Crunch, an eventuality reflected poetically in the New Testament: 'The heavens will be dissolved in flames and the elements melted by fire.' [1] There is more than poetry here. The sun shines because it burns up its hydrogen fuel to form helium in the process of nuclear fusion. In another five thousand million years or so, some scientists say, this hydrogen will be used up and all life on earth will be destroyed.

The world has evolved from raw energy to ninety-two different chemicals, to the first living cell, to viruses, bacteria, fish, birds, and animals and ultimately to the appearance of human beings on the planet.

We humans have evolved within a complex network of natural forces that obey their own laws. When, for example, human male sperm penetrates the female egg, the human body begins to take shape according to the laws of nature. The body is a miracle not because it defies the laws of nature, but precisely because it obeys them. Our digestive systems extract nutrients from food. Our skins help to regulate body temperature. When we get sick, our bodies have built-in defence mechanisms to fight the illness. The food we eat, the climate that shapes us, the materials for the clothes we wear, even our ways of thinking, are all products of forces and influences that have been at work over millennia. All these wonderful things happen, usually without our being aware of them, in accordance with the laws of nature. However while nature may produce the beauty of flowers, sunsets, mountains, rivers, lakes and seas, not to mention the wondrous birth of a child, it also produces earthquakes, tidal waves, heart attacks, cancers, physical and mental disabilities and death. The fact is that we could not survive on the planet without the laws of nature but that means that we have to live with their potential dangers also.

As we think about the great evolutionary process that has been going on for millions of years, we gradually become aware that we are part of something that is greater than ourselves, that we can never make fully our own. We are part of the ' stream of life' and this sense of being part of some great evolutionary movement can give rise to a sense of wonder, mystery and awe. It can also tell us something of the grandeur and mystery of God.

God did not simply create the universe millions of years ago and then leave it to its own devices. At every moment of its existence God 'births' the energy that moves the evolutionary process forward from the unfathomable network of forces that move the tiniest atom in its inner dynamism to the vast galaxies in their cycles as they become separate and individual.

God, out of love, creates what is 'other' than God – sets in motion, in a time-scale that is unimaginably enormous, an evolutionary process that profligately gives birth to the cosmos and to our own tiny planet. 'We know that all creation is groaning in labour pains even until now.'[2]

We may feel, of course, that if we were in charge of creation we would manage it better. We would retain the good and eliminate the bad! However, the balance and relatedness of all things shows that it is not as easy as we might suppose to make such changes if the universe is to remain subject to its own underlying lawful regularity enabling the human species to survive. Of course it is possible to conceive of a world in which God intervened on every occasion cancer cells formed so as to eliminate the disease by direct action: possible but difficult to conceive if that world is to be rational and orderly instead of magical and capricious. However, it may be that the way that God creates the world reflects God's character in some way.

why is it better to be rational and orderly? [margin note]

Polkinghorne [margin note]

'The world that science describes seems to me to be one that is consonant with the idea that it is the expression of the will of a Creator, subtle, patient and content to achieve his purposes by the slow unfolding of process inherent in those laws of nature which, in their regularity, are but pale reflections of his abiding faithfulness.'[3]

Pace Shakespeare, the world is not a stage but *a process* in which everything that exists, has existed or will exist is intrinsically interdependent. We are linked symbiotically not only to the impersonal flow of nature but also to all other living beings, to others and to God. Even our names are given to us, symbolising the fact that we are descendent from and dependent on others for our very existence.

While we tend to think of ourselves as unique, as separate individuals over against nature and other people, it is only in and through our relationships with others that we become persons. Inextricably linked to others, we are also inextricably linked to the impersonal flow of the natural world. As an individual, one never outgrows this basic solidarity with everything and everyone else. Our lives are always personal and inter-personal and because, and only because, we are linked to planet earth do we exist at all.

Sara Maitland makes the point that 'if the cosmos, matter itself, exists in love, rather than from some bureaucratic or edifying purpose, it can, indeed it must, be free to grow, develop, evolve, change, experiment – profligately, extravagantly, randomly. The first ping into being of the first hydrogen atom *ex nihilo*, unthinkable and violently radical though that was, cannot be enough for love – any more than looking at a new-born baby, or spotting someone seriously fanciable at a party can be enough; you desire the thing or person you love to display more and more of what it is to be, what they are in the process of becoming, to change and grow and respond. It is only in this context of this extraordinary activity that we can truly rejoice in the generosity of our God; that we can live free from fear; that we can choose love and participation and joy; that we can realise what we have truly been given.'[4]

But we are still left with the basic question of how to (*) reconcile human suffering in all its ugliness with a God of love. One of the problems is that God seems to be above and beyond human suffering. Classical theology, based on Greek thought, speaks of God as unmoved Pure Being. It says that God cannot suffer or be directly affected by suffering. Even when speaking of Jesus, classical theology will say that he suffered only in his human nature, not in his divine nature.

Furthermore, God is said to be omnipotent, in ultimate control of whatever happens and nothing that happens is outside God's will. The fact that suffering and evil are not prevented by God means, not that God wills them directly, but that God permits them to happen for some purpose; to punish wrongdoing, to test character, to educate or form personality or to bring about some greater good. But it is hard to see how suffering that destroys the lives of very young children, for example, is a just punishment, tests character, educates in any way, or brings about some greater good. There is even a radical suffering that affects people so that they no longer exercise any freedom, feel any affection, have any hope or feel any love.

The idea of God being unaffected by the barbarous excesses of human suffering simply cannot be tolerated. If God could stop all this suffering but does not, how can

God be called good or loving? A God who is unaffected by human pain hardly merits love and affection in return. A God who stands by and simply 'permits' evil is hardly worthy of love or praise.

However, the God of Jesus Christ is not some lofty, apathetic deity but a compassionate God, rejoicing in our joys and suffering with us when we suffer but, of course, *in ways far beyond our understanding.* 'God is love and who-ever remains in love remains in God,' the first letter of John tells us. Love is giving and receiving in mutual rela-tionships. Love means being open to others, sharing one-self with them, allowing oneself to be vulnerable to others' experience, rejoicing with them in their joys and grieving with them in their sorrows. Such is the very essence of love. God's love, if it is to mean anything at all, must mean (✻) that God is vulnerable in some unfathomable way and re-joices and suffers with us also.

Perhaps the best place to see God's involvement with suffering humanity is on Calvary where Jesus endured that most violent, disgraceful, scandalous, shocking and gruesome form of execution known to the ancient world, crucifixion.

(✻) he should pick up on kenosis here, esp. in J.Polkinghorne

CHAPTER 2

Calvary

In the human integrity of Jesus, one who valued truth and fidelity above his own life and loved his friends even to the end, something of the mystery of God's involvement in suffering humanity becomes clear. On the cross we see God participating in the suffering of the world and over-coming it from within through the power of love.

Jesus is 'the radiant light of God's glory and the perfect copy of his nature.'[5] 'Whoever has seen me has seen the Father,' Jesus said.[6] To see Jesus enduring the agony of crucifixion is to see someone who embodies God suffering with us. God, in Jesus, voluntarily sets aside divinity and enters into the human condition and therefore into the evolutionary process itself. God enters human darkness and weakness in order to transform it from within and bring life out of death. To see Christ on the cross is to see a suffering God who enters our history, our agonies, and our crucifixions. In Christ's suffering and dying God compas-sionately suffered and continues to suffer with all men and women of all times and all ages in their on-going agonies. 'I was hungry and you never gave me food; I was thirsty and you never gave me drink; I was a stranger and you never made me welcome, naked and you never clothed me, sick and in prison and you never visited me.'[7] A God who is not in some way affected by human suffering is not really worthy to stake a claim to our love.

God enters into the agonies of men and women today just as God entered into the sufferings of Jesus. So it was for Etty, a young Dutch Jewess who poured out her heart to God in her diary as the Holocaust descended on her race: 'One thing is becoming increasingly clear to me: that you cannot help us; that we must help you to help ourselves. That is all we can manage these days and also all that matters: that we safeguard that little piece of you, God, in ourselves.'[8]

Or as Margaret Spufford, a mother with a severely handicapped child, put it: 'One of the most helpful things that was ever said to me was that the definition of "Almighty" means that there is no evil out of which good cannot be brought. This I have found, extremely painfully, to be true. The fundamentally awry can perhaps never be made whole in this life; yet like the twisted tree, or the (twisted) child's courage and wisdom, it can take on a beauty of its own. And in this transformation, the constant presence of an enabling God seems to be vital. My image of a Creator in whose creation there are mistakes not logically comprehensible may be true, but it has to be extended into the image of a Creator who ceaselessly, patiently, works to transform and re-create what has gone amiss, above all in his own entry into this creation to amend and redeem it. Some of this re-creation and patient transformation of what has gone amiss I can myself bear witness to.'[9]

The presence of a compassionate, companioning, enabling God does not make evil any less evil or diminish human suffering, but it can bring a deep down consolation and comfort. Just as there is great comfort for a sick child held in its mother's arms, so God does not stand outside suffering or peer down on it from on high. God is present in the grief, in the shame, in the hopelessness, in the agony. God is in and with the sufferer, submerged in the experience. Being aware of God's presence in human agony can help soothe the wounded spirit. Knowing that God shares our suffering enables us to bear the pain. Such communion can become a deep source of energy for bearing one's suffering and for resisting evil. Knowing that God is with us makes all the difference.

Jesus' life is a paradigm for discovering how God is involved in the suffering of humanity. Jesus knew in the depths of his heart that he was the beloved of God. Nothing, even suffering and death, could separate him from that love: it gave him the courage and strength to bear all. We too are beloved of God. When we return love for love we participate in God's very life. The deeper that union the more we will be able to bear suffering and pain because we know in the depths of our hearts that nothing can separate us from our loving God and that the fullness of love awaits us.

Who knows the mind of God? Who knows why God creates the cosmos or our tiny world? Followers of Christ, of course, believe that whatever God does is done out of love. In creating a world that enables human existence and human choice, God's very self is open to the precariousness of evolution and of human choosing. God's loving act of creation implies a self-limiting and a self-emptying which allows the vulnerability implicit in all creative acts to impinge on God's own being. Just as a woman, while owning a powerful sense of creativity and joy, often gives birth in pain and suffering, so does God in whose image we are created. 'I will cry out like a woman in labour, I will gasp and pant.'[10]

God's vulnerability comes from his love. Because God loves us, God does not coerce us or generally interfere with the laws of nature. What God can and does do is to enter into our suffering, sustaining us by his love, often mediated through others – doctors, nurses, parents, helpers – enabling us to cope, if we trust him, 'because neither life nor death, trouble or hardship, persecution or hunger, poverty or danger can separate us from the love of God. In all these things we have victory through him who loves us.'[11]

Over the course of human history God 'births' human beings capable of returning love for love. Humanity will finally reach maturity only in the promised new heaven and new earth when evolution and human history have finally run their course. The question remains, however, as to whether God's power could not have saved humanity from all the suffering and pain that people have to endure.

Power is the basic energy that is needed to initiate and sustain action, translating intention into reality. Throughout history power has tended to imply insensitivity, cruelty, control, domination and oppression. The reality is that power is implicit in every human interaction – familial, sexual, occupational, national or international, either covertly or overtly. When one thinks of power one tends to think of something or someone who is 'above', dominating, controlling or oppressing us. People often think of God like that.

God's power is different. God's power is 'from below'. God's power is neither power over people or powerlessness but power 'with' people. God's power is not the power of control through either domination or benevolence but the power of love that operates by persuasion. God's power is *empowerment*, a liberating power of connectedness that becomes effective in the lives of men and women through mutual love. God's power is the power of attraction, inviting us to go beyond our limitations, as well as the limitations imposed upon us by the laws of nature which are necessary for our very existence. God invites us to accept that we are loved no matter who we are or whatever pain or suffering we have to endure.

God's power engenders hope because it enables men and women to struggle against all forms of powerlessness, oppression, suffering and pain, in the knowledge that the struggle will never be in vain. God's power is a power that saves. While the Bible is quite clear that salvation is God's work, it also points out that salvation is our responsibility as human beings. We have to make decisions and take action; otherwise there is no salvation. There would have been no freedom for the Hebrew slaves in Egypt, for example, if they had not taken the decision to follow Moses through the Sea of Reeds. God has gifted all that we have and all that we are to us: in that sense God is ultimately our Saviour. But we have to use our God-given freedom creatively to 'work out our salvation with fear and trembling.'[12]

We are shapers of our own history, not merely the object of other peoples' or even of God's control. God's salvation appears when we begin to use the gifts that God has given us and start taking responsibility for our own lives and our own future. We are, in a sense, co-creators. We build (or fail to build) a world in which we can give each other the courage and the ability to shape our own history. As Sara Maitland has noted, mothers create the child's self but the child also creates the mother for a woman cannot be a mother without the child, or a father without a son or daughter. Carers exist because they care for someone and that someone creates the carer. While some who are cared for may be totally dependent on others for all their physical needs, they are nonetheless being creative by evoking love in those who look after them. In God's scheme of things, love is always the key.

CHAPTER 3

Living in Hope

A God who is capable of suffering in compassionate love opens up a future in the midst of suffering. Because God is God, nothing is ultimately more powerful than God's love and so there are limits to what suffering and evil can do. We can go forward in hope knowing that God's compassionate love will overcome all suffering and evil, even death itself. This hope is founded on the central mystery of Christian faith, the death and resurrection of Jesus. 'God raised the Lord and will also raise us by his power.'[13] The New Testament promises not 'immortality of the soul', a concept unknown to the Israelites, but restoration of the whole person. This is why Christian teaching speaks of the resurrection of the body, not just survival of some tenuous part called the soul but a reconstitution of the whole person in an environment of God's choosing.

While we have no direct experience of resurrection, there are human analogies which may give us a glimpse of what resurrection might look like: the joy of reunion with loved ones after long separation; new beginnings after extreme failure and disappointment: growth towards acceptance and light following the shock and depression following a serious heart attack.

What Jesus promises is fullness of life centred on God where we are united with everyone and everything else in recognisable continuity with our lives now. All of creation, human history, culture, even the scars of our sufferings will be present but in a transfigured way 'in the end time'. We will be invited into a new world of relationships which will exceed by far the wildest dreams we have of knowing and being known, of loving and being loved. As Father, Son and Spirit are transparent to one another, so will we be without any diminution of our individuality or otherness.

Perhaps, out of a sense of security, we would prefer to have a God who is king and judge, even a tyrant; one who is in absolute control, one who solves all our problems for us, like the mother and father of our childhood. But does such a God not reflect our immaturity, our fear of human vulnerability, of letting go in love? Somehow a vulnerable God seems to be a defective God. However, the God of Jesus, while vulnerable, is strong through the power of love and 'wanders with Israel through the dust of the streets and hangs on the gallows of Auschwitz' (Jürgen Moltmann).

'The SS seemed more preoccupied, more disturbed than usual. To hang a young boy in front of thousands of spectators was no light matter. The head of the camp read the verdict. All eyes were on the child. He was lividly pale, almost calm, biting his lips. The gallows threw its shadow over him ... the three victims mounted together onto the chairs. The three necks were placed at the same moment within the nooses. "Long live liberty", cried the two adults.

But the child was silent. "Where is God? Where is He?" someone behind me asked. At a sign from the head of the camp, the three chairs tipped over. Total silence throughout the camp. On the horizon the sun was setting. "Bare your heads!" yelled the head of the camp. His voice was raucous. We were weeping. "Cover your heads." Then the march past began. The two adults were no longer alive. Their tongues hung swollen, blue-tinged. But the third rope was still moving: being so light, the child was still alive. For more than half an hour he stayed there, struggling between life and death, dying in slow agony under our eyes. And we had to look at him full in the face. He was still alive when I passed in front of him. His tongue was still red, his eyes not yet glazed. Behind me I heard the same man asking: "Where is God now?" And I heard a voice within me answer him: "Where is he? Here he is – he is hanging here on the gallows."'[14]

God, in the unfathomable and mysterious depths of his being, suffers our pains and defeats, enters into them and still remains God. This may seem like nonsense because 'the message about Christ on the cross is nonsense to those who are being lost; but for us who are being saved it is God's power. The scripture says, "I will destroy the wisdom of the wise and set aside the understanding of the scholars." So then, where does that leave the wise? Or the scholars? Or the skilful debaters of this world? God has shown that this world's wisdom is foolishness. For what seems to be God's foolishness is wiser than human wisdom, and what seems to be God's weakness is stronger than human strength.'[15]

To speak of God suffering out of compassionate love for humanity is not to make of suffering something of value in itself. Nor does it mean that God is essentially weak or powerless. To hold such a view would be to deny the value of peoples' struggles for equality, dignity and the fullness of humanity and to deny the real power of God who has showered his gifts on us so that we can have life and have it to the full. One way that those who wish to keep others in subjection employ is to inculcate a feeling of powerlessness in those who are oppressed. Unless people come to know their own God-given power through questioning the oppressor's values and assumptions and struggling with others against the imposed structures that make them victims, they will have no energy to resist. Therefore, an image of a helpless God will only strengthen their sense of helplessness in the struggle for freedom, self-affirmation and autonomy.

To speak, however, about redemptive suffering and the

power of a suffering God are of immense benefit to those who know suffering from the inside. God's suffering is an expression of his love, in that it flows out of his care and compassion for broken humanity.

There can be a certain sentimentality in our view of God's creative love. We can forget that anger and even wrath are attributed to God in both the Jewish and Christian Testaments. God's anger is the other side of the coin of God's love and is born of compassion for those who are sinned against, those who are oppressed, those women, children and men whose lives are violated and degraded.

Suffering and death, where we reach our extreme limits, force us to ask basic questions about the sense or non-sense of life. Either we die into nothingness or we die into the mysterious, incomprehensible reality we call God. Neither of these convictions is 'provable'; they are both, like love itself, a matter of faith, of trust. Moments of suffering and dying become crucial tests of our belief in God, of whether we are prepared to trust God or not. Are we prepared to trust that God, who is Absolute Love, will fulfil all the longings of our hearts with a love that endures or will they simply fade into oblivion?

'Everything is possible for the person who has faith,' Jesus said.[16] The faith he was talking about was not simply a belief in dogmas and doctrines but trust in God's love and God's word. Jesus said, 'For truly I tell you, if you have faith the size of a mustard seed, you will say to this mountain "move from here to there", and it will move; and nothing will be impossible for you.'[17] Jesus saw faith as a mighty power, something that could achieve the impossible, like moving mountains! Faith is the conviction that goodness will eventually triumph over evil: it is the conviction that God will prevail in spite of all the suffering and evil in the world that seem to indicate otherwise.

Christ's parable of the mustard seed, usually understood

as a symbol of the gradual development of faith from small beginnings to a thriving relationship with God, can help us to understand how God is present and active in moments of suffering and pain. When we experience any of the crucifixions that afflict the human spirit we experience something of what the mystics call the Dark Night of the Soul. Interiorly and exteriorly, our senses are being purified and emptied. We have nothing left to hold on to and we feel that there is nothing more we can take.

Up to this point we were able to cope with life. We could defend and protect ourselves and live life more or less as we wanted. But then we reach a crisis point and slowly and painfully, willingly or unwillingly, we surrender control. We are in utter darkness, stripped of anything to hold on to. Nothing seems to be left and it seems that not even God can save us.

Such moments invite us to plunge more deeply into God, to let go of everything and surrender to the only One who can save us. 'Do not be afraid, for I have redeemed you; I have called you by name, you are mine.'[18] These consoling words are fertile ground for a renewed sense of God's presence.

Love is real, the greatest reality of human existence. Despite our sufferings and pain, Love can gradually take hold of us. 'Should you pass through the sea, I will be with you.' Love's silent but faithful presence can sustain us and gradually free us so that we can let go of all those things we thought we could never do without – country, home, family and friends, our successes, our health and even life itself. Why? Because Love is at the very centre of our being calling us back into the Love-Event that is God and because in God we will find once more, burnished and transfigured, all that we thought we had lost.

The mustard seed of faith grows and flourishes if we allow ourselves to experience the peace and joy of knowing that we are eternally loved and will live forever in

Love. While God does not dispense us from the forces that are at play in our evolving world, God does provide an overpowering energy that can come to us if we join ourselves to God's power of love 'as rays of light from the sun and as waters from their fountains'.[19] Our actual faith experience may seem very small, like a tiny mustard seed, but moments of crisis can make us turn to Love as the vital centre of all that we are and hope to become. Sometimes our experience of God is like the seed growing silently.[20] At other times it bursts into full bloom so that God becomes the sustaining source for all we cherish and hope for.

People say that they cannot believe in God because there is so much suffering in the world. Perhaps the opposite is the case. It is only if there is a God that we can avoid the depths of despair and face human suffering in all of its horrifying reality, conscious of the fact that there is a God who summons us, walks with us, sustains us with his transforming presence *in and through suffering* to the ultimate fulfilment of all human longing and to fullness of life.

Suffering is not a sign of God's absence. When we, or those we love, suffer it may seem as if we have been forsaken by God. We may even echo the cry of Jesus on the cross, 'My God, my God, why have you forsaken me?' We cannot avoid suffering but we can find a way through it. What we have to endure, however, can become a way of encountering God as Jesus did in the midst of his own suffering when he exclaimed, 'Father, into your hands I commend my spirit.'

CHAPTER 4

An Eye for an Eye

After the horrific terrorist attacks of 11 September 2001 in New York, Washington and Pennsylvania, voices were raised calling for revenge on those who carried out these terrible atrocities, echoing in many ways a saying from the Jewish scriptures: 'Anyone who maims another shall suffer the same injury in return: fracture for fracture, eye for eye, tooth for tooth; the injury inflicted is the injury to be suffered.'[21] While the Ten Commandments state 'you shall not kill,'[22] God is also quoted in the Bible as saying 'Whoever strikes a man a mortal blow must be put to death.'[23] 'Whoever strikes father or mother shall be put to death. A kidnapper, whether he sells his victim or still has him when caught, shall be put to death. Whoever curses his father or mother shall be put to death.'[24] 'The Lord said to Moses, "This man (who was discovered gathering wood on the Sabbath day while the Israelites were still in the desert) shall be put to death; let the whole community stone him outside the camp,"'[25] and so on and so forth.

How can one reconcile a loving and ever-forgiving God, as portrayed by Jesus, with some of these commands attributed to God in the Old Testament? If God exists, is he nothing more than a vengeful God?

To understand these sayings attributed to God one has to place them in context. The Bible is said to be the inspired word of God, meaning that it comes from God, or is related to God in some special way. Although we speak of the Bible in the singular, it is in fact a collection of some seventy books, written at different times and in different places.

These books contain 'inspired' poetry, drama, legend, parable and history which, *in their varying ways*, tell us something of *'that truth which God, for the sake of our salvation, wished to see confided to the sacred scriptures.'*[26]

It is important to be clear about what we mean when we say that God 'inspires' the authors of the various books in the Bible. When it refers to God 'speaking' to Moses, for example, it does not mean that God whispered in his ear or gave him some sort of mental dictation and that he literally wrote down what God had said. The scriptural writings are human compositions: the words were chosen by human beings, composed within a particular society, influenced by the underlying culture and moral values of that society, as well as by the culture and values of neighbouring societies.

As Vatican Two pointed out, 'the fact is that truth is differently presented and expressed in the various types of historical writing, in prophetical and poetical texts, and in other forms of literary expression. Hence the exegete, (one who offers critical explanations of scripture) must look for that meaning which the sacred writers, in given situations and granted the circumstances of their time and culture, intended to express and did in fact express, through the medium of a contemporary literary form. Rightly to understand what the sacred authors wanted to affirm in their work, due attention must be paid both to the customary and characteristic patterns of perception, speech and narrative which prevailed in their time, and to the conventions which people then observed in their dealings with one another.'[27]

The question of slavery may help us to understand something about God's 'inspiration'. Up to the nineteenth century slavery was widely accepted by many in society. However, as men and women began to reflect on what slavery meant and what it did to human beings, they began to realise how inhumane it was until finally it was abolished, at least in law! One could say that these men and women were 'inspired' by God's Spirit as they began to understand the inhumanity of slavery and sought to have it abolished.

In somewhat similar fashion, Moses was 'inspired' by God to lead his people out of slavery in Egypt and discover and proclaim ways of living that would make for a more human and humane society and unite Israel more closely to God. This does not mean that Moses or the prophets had the answer to every human and scientific problem that would face humanity in succeeding generations because they were, like all of us, people of their time, bound by the customs, conventions and mind-set that they used in their dealings with one another.

The more we recognise that the Bible is a human composition, using human words and different literary styles, the more we can recognise the combination of the truly divine and the truly human in the scriptures. The story of Jonah and the big fish, for example, is a parable and not history – an inspired parable concerning God's mercy. Inspiration does not mean that we have to accept that a historical figure called Jonah was actually swallowed by a large fish! Similarly the story of creation in the book of Genesis is not a scientific description of the origins of the world but rather an imaginary, poetic picture gleaned from various myths that the author used to convey the truth that God is the creator of the universe and all that is in it. Hence there is no contradiction between acceptance of God's inspiration on the one hand and the acceptance of different literary forms or styles in the Bible on the other.

Unlike the many tribes around them who worshipped multiple gods, the Israelites came to believe in one God. Worship of the one God united the various tribes of Israel and gave them their sense of identity. Anything that undermined that sense of identity was seen as blasphemy against God and could even lead to the unleashing of a contagious cycle of reciprocal violence and a fundamental breakdown of society.

As the various tribes of Israel tried to gain greater cohesion, the prophets and leaders of Israel were 'inspired' by God, guided by God's Spirit, often through some form of mystical experience, which is described by the analogy of speech and hearing. This inspiration enabled Israel's leaders and prophets to discover how people should behave in their inter-personal and inter-tribal relationships and how they should relate to God. However, this was an ever-evolving voyage of discovery that the biblical authors tried to communicate in many different literary forms.

In the light of what we have said, we can return to our initial question about how to reconcile the notion of a God of love with some of the commands attributed to God in the Jewish Testament. One convention in primitive times, including the early periods of Israel's history, was the use of religion to tame, direct, and virtually control violence. Before the advent of juridical systems, religion allowed a limited form of violence in order to avoid the disaster of unleashing a contagious cycle of reciprocal violence.

'An eye for an eye and a tooth for a tooth' was seen as preferable to the wholesale slaughter of a neighbouring tribe because of some injury done to one's own tribe. The command, therefore, was meant to moderate vengeance: the punishment should not exceed the injury done. Those who injured others or killed them or undermined the basic values that gave the Israelites their sense of identity were seen as 'blaspheming' against God and such people were liable either to be ostracised by the community or put to death for more serious breaches of the covenant relationship with God.

While the command of 'an eye for an eye and a tooth for a tooth' was meant to moderate vengeance, Jesus forbade even this proportionate retaliation. 'You have heard that it was said, "An eye for an eye and a tooth for a tooth." But I say to you, offer no resistance to the one who is evil. When someone strikes you on your right cheek, turn the other one to him as well.'[28] Jesus' teaching is radical and goes against the natural tendency to seek revenge. 'But I say to you that listen, love your enemies, do good to those who hate you, bless those who curse you, pray for those who abuse you. If anyone strikes you on the cheek, offer the other also; and from the one who takes away your coat do not withhold your shirt. Give to everyone who begs from you, and if anyone takes away your goods, do not ask for them again. Do to others as you would have them do to you.'[29]

Jesus teaches non-resistance to evil in the sense of avoiding physical violence but leaving open the possibility of psychological or moral resistance as exemplified, for example, by Mahatma Gandhi or Martin Luther King. Jesus' teaching is a strategy for winning, not for passive resignation or indifference to evil. The greatest commandment is love of God and neighbour,[30] and Jesus extends this commandment of love even to one's enemies and persecutors. Jesus could hardly have used more effective words by way of shocking people into the realisation that he wished all men and women to be part of God's inclusive love.

St Paul echoed the same sentiments when he wrote: 'Beloved, do not look for revenge but leave room for the wrath; for it is written, "Vengeance is mine, I will repay, says the Lord." Rather if your enemy is hungry, feed him; if he is thirsty, give him something to drink; for by doing so you will heap burning coals upon his head. Do not be conquered by evil but conquer evil by good.'[31]

Love of ones' enemies, as well as love of God and neighbour, is central to Jesus' teaching, But who is this Jesus: just a good man or someone who was divine? As he once asked his disciples as they set out for the villages of Caesarea Philippi, 'Who do you say that I am?'

PART 2

Who is Jesus?

Jesus and his disciples set out for the villages of Caesarea Philippi. Along the way he asked his disciples, 'Who do people say that I am?' They said in reply, 'John the Baptist, others Elijah, still others one of the prophets.' And he asked them, 'But who do *you* say that I am?'

(Mark 8:27-29)

CHAPTER 5

Who is Jesus?

Christians find themselves in a period of transition from a homogeneous church, largely integrated into secular culture and society, to a church as a group of believers living in the midst of people who question the relevance of religion to modern living and, denying the divinity of Jesus, see him simply as one of the commanding figures of history.

In this chapter I want to look at what we can say about Jesus with some degree of historical accuracy. Who was he? Where did he come from? Why did he set out on a mission to Israel? In subsequent chapters I examine the central elements of his teaching and then go on to examine the meaning and significance of his resurrection, of his role as saviour of the world and whether we can believe in his miracles.

Historically we can know something, if not a great deal, about his birth and infancy, and some facts can be affirmed with at least some degree of probability.[1] He was born, perhaps in Bethlehem, but most likely in Nazareth somewhere around 7-4 BCE. (For theological reasons, the gospel writers may have placed his birth in Bethlehem, the city of David.) His mother was named Miryam (Mary) and his putative father was called Yosef (Joseph). It was said that he was a descendant of King David. The reason for such a claim was that Joseph, who was regarded as his legal father, was of the lineage of King David. Jesus grew up in Nazareth and was so identified with that town that he was called Jesus the Nazarene.

Jesus probably spoke Aramaic as his main language

though there is reason to believe that he knew biblical
Hebrew and possibly some Greek, which was the language often used in trade in the bigger towns of the time. It
is reasonable to suppose that his religious formation included instruction in reading biblical Hebrew. As the first-
born son, Jesus would have learned his father's trade but
would also have been taught the religious traditions and
texts of Judaism. His skill, as an adult, in debating with the
Scribes, Pharisees and Jerusalem authorities argue for
some degree of reading knowledge of the sacred texts. He
may even have received some primary education in the
synagogue in Nazareth. If this is so, we can well understand
the reaction of his peers and elders when he later returned
to teach there. 'When the Sabbath came he began to teach
in the synagogue, and many who heard him were astonished. They said, "Where did this man get all this? What
kind of wisdom has been given to him? What mighty
deeds are wrought by his hands! Is he not the carpenter,
the son of Mary, and the brother of James and Joseph and
Judas and Simon? Are not his sisters here with us?" And
they took offence at him.'[2] In other words, they were saying, 'who does he think he is?'

Jesus plied his trade as a woodworker. He would have
done work in carpentry making beds, tables, stools and
lamp stands, plows and yokes, but he probably did some
work in stone as well. While he would have had to work
hard for his living, Jesus was probably no poorer or less re-
spectable than anyone else in Nazareth or in the rest of
Galilee for that matter. There is no reason to believe that he
suffered from the grinding, degrading poverty of the day
labourer or the rural salve. He worked as a tradesman, a
calling involving a broad range of skills demanding much
sweat and muscle power, hardly the weakling often presented in pious paintings!

So, for the first thirty years of his life, Jesus lived quietly
in Nazareth, a village of between one thousand six hun-

dred and two thousand people. He was known simply as the woodworker's son. His life was unexceptional until he decided to leave Nazareth and undertake a mission to Israel. At that point his family and neighbours must have been shocked. There was nothing in his previous life that seemed to foreshadow what was to come. So, we must ask, what made him give up his trade, leave his family and village life and begin a new career as an itinerant preacher?

One of the major influences in Jesus' decision to leave Nazareth may well have been the preaching of John the Baptist. Jesus knew of John's life in the wilderness and of his prophetic message and there was much of it with which he agreed. John taught that the end of Israel's history was fast approaching: that Israel had abandoned God's ways and so the people were in imminent danger of being consumed by God's wrathful judgment. (The holiness of God automatically reacts against all that is not holy in Israel's conduct, especially any apostasy and idolatry that breaks the covenant relationship with God.) John said that, to avoid God's wrath, the people would have to pass from their present sinful state by having a change of mind, heart and conduct, (conversion) sealed by undergoing ritual immersion (baptism) administered by John himself.

Jesus continued the prophetic mission of John but saw things somewhat differently.[3] Like John he proclaimed repentance and the need for conversion.[4] He too demanded a turning away from old ways and a change of mind, heart and behaviour, or else God's judgment would overtake Israel. But, in contrast to John who threatened imminent disaster on the people of Israel, Jesus came with a message of salvation and mercy. He proclaimed a vision of righteousness, love, mercy, forgiveness and freedom.

Jesus drew companions to himself, including some who had been disciples of John the Baptist. He set up a group within his circle of friends whom he called the Twelve, symbolising the original twelve tribes of Israel, thereby indicating that his mission was to re-gather the whole of the house of Israel and make it once more, both in word and deed, God's holy people. He moved from town to town healing and 'casting out demons'. He engaged in religious disputes with other devout Jews and presumed to teach them how to observe the Mosaic Law properly. He taught his disciples special forms of prayer and beliefs that marked them off from their coreligionists. He was also unusual in that he attracted a following from among women of both high and low social status and made friends with 'outcasts' such as tax collectors and 'sinners', those who were unable to fulfill all the requirements of the Law.

Like John, Jesus proclaimed the imminent end of history. He emphasised the urgency of the choices he was offering people by pointing out the dire consequences of not accepting his message. All of this reflected the life and preaching of John and, while there were some notable shifts of emphasis in Jesus' teaching, John's teaching was clearly seminal.

Mindful of the history of suffering that his people endured, Jesus set out on a mission of liberation and reconciliation to 'the lost sheep of the house of Israel.'[5] Leaving the Baptist, he struck out on his own, proclaiming God's imminent yet present kingdom. The kingdom of God was absolutely central to all that Jesus said and did. If we are to understand him and what he was about, we have to be clear what he meant when he taught his disciples to pray 'Thy kingdom come'.

CHAPTER 6

The Kingdom of God

I have a dream that one day this nation will rise up and live out the true meaning of its creed: 'We hold these truths to be self-evident, that all men are created equal.'

I have a dream that one day on the red hills of Georgia the sons of former slaves and the sons of former slave-owners will be able to sit down together at the table of brotherhood.

I have a dream that my four little children will one day live in a nation where they will not be judged by the colour of their skin but by the content of their character.

(Martin Luther King)

Just as Martin Luther King electrified a crowd of 200,000 people with his famous 'I have a Dream' speech in September 1963, so, if we read the Jewish and Christian Testaments carefully, God can electrify us with his dream for humanity.

In creating the universe in all its complexity and beauty, including the millions of human beings who ever have or will inhabit mother earth, God had a dream, a single intention. God's dream was to create a world where all human beings could live as brothers and sisters in a community of faith, hope and love, united by God's Spirit with Jesus Christ as sons and daughters of God, our one Father, and in harmony with the whole created universe. Paul expressed the same idea when he wrote; 'The Father of Our Lord Jesus Christ ... has made known to us in all wisdom and insight the mystery of his will, according to his purpose which he set forth in Christ as a plan for the fullness of time, to unite all things in him, things in heaven and things on earth.'[6]

God, desiring to share his life, his love and his creative abilities, creates the universe and this act of creation includes all the freely determined actions of every human being. This is why the future of God's creative action is not yet fully determined – it depends on how human beings react to God's initiative. Our actions can be in tune, or out of tune, with God's dream for the world.

Jesus was deeply aware of how people were out of tune with God's dream. He noted the behaviour of those in authority and how they kept the masses in poverty and fear, using the Law for their own aggrandisement. He felt a deep compassion for the outcasts of his day: the poor, the oppressed, beggars, the blind, the deaf, cripples, unskilled labourers, widows and orphans. He was determined to do something about their plight. But what could be done? Revolt against the Roman imperialists and their collaborators? No, because 'all who draw the sword will die by the sword.'[7] Jesus believed in a different, more demanding way. What had to be done, he said, was to pray for the coming of the kingdom or reign of God on earth. He desired that all would accept God's reign and live accordingly.

What Jesus was calling for was nothing less than the transformation of the culture of his time. A culture is a process that is actively at work within a people, often in an unconscious way. It characterises a people through the different ways they relate to one another and to the world in which they live. A culture is inherited from the past but also changes and adapts in order to cope with different moments of history and different environments. Culture evolves into a selective set of assumptions, often unconsciously assimilated within a given society. It involves an entire way of life shared by people and, as such, is a source of their solidarity and identity. It involves ways of interpreting the world by carrying and expressing meaning and beliefs, norms for behaviour, customs and traditions. Cultural expressions frequently embody themselves in institutions and systems which preserve those meanings and values, or in symbolic forms such as a handshake, a flag, a ritual etc.[8] When Jesus prayed for the coming of God's kingdom, he was, in effect, praying for a profound change in Jewish culture.

The word 'kingdom' can present certain difficulties because, over the centuries, it has taken on connotations that we have to try to shake off. It smacks of monarchy and absolutist rule. Some people today prefer to use the term 'the reign of God' because kingdom seems to refer to a place, like the United Kingdom, the Kingdom of Spain or 'heaven'. Christ's understanding was very different. 'Heaven' in the New Testament is simply a synonym for God: the kingdom of heaven and the kingdom of God mean the same thing.

Jesus saw the kingdom as coming about on earth. Indeed to pray 'thy kingdom come' is the same as praying 'thy will be done on earth'. When Jesus, for example, said 'My kingdom is not of this world,[9] he did not mean to imply that it is or will be located somewhere else, in a life after death for example. What he meant was that God's kingdom, God's reign in human hearts, involves living according to a different set of values from those normally found in the world. The kingdom comes about on earth when people are in tune with God's dream and, overcoming mutual fear and distrust, pursue the paths of peace, truth, justice and love in their relationships.

For Jesus the kingdom of God was a paradigm of what life should be like and of what it will look like at the end of history, 'in the fullness of time'. He was trying to put into words how the world would be different if God were to reign in human hearts, if God's dream for humanity was fully taken on board. Jesus' words and actions challenged people. He called them to 'repentance', that is to ways of thinking and acting that are in tune with God's dream for humanity. He prayed that God's reign would become a reality so that his people would be able to face God's final judgement.

God, Jesus said, wants men and women to be 'in communion' with one another, to live as brothers and sisters, sons and daughters of a loving Father, in a world where there is no war, no domination of one group by another, no rich and no poor, no oppressors and oppressed, no famine and plenty side by side. He wanted a world where all would be one as Jesus and his Father are one.[10] For such a world to exist, all human relationships – inter-personal, social, religious, cultural, political or economic – would have to undergo change. God reigns where relationships are so structured that a new, transformed society comes into being.

Can such a state of affairs ever be attained in our 'dog-eat-dog' world? Surely it is naïve to believe that all men and women can become brothers and sisters? The only possible reply is the one given by Jesus. 'For human beings it is impossible, but not for God. All things are possible for God.'[11] Yes, it is difficult to share God's dream but not impossible. Human beings can attune themselves to God's dream by heeding Jesus' call to conversion and praying that whatever hinders them from living out that dream, whatever fears prevent them from living as sisters and brothers, will be overcome by God's graceful initiative.

How God's reign comes about is often mysterious and can happen in extraordinary ways. Jesus illustrates this point with two short parables. 'The Kingdom of God is like yeast that a woman took and mixed with three measures of wheat flour until the whole batch was leavened.'[12] A small amount of yeast, mixed with three measures of wheat, is enough to feed a hundred people. The conversion of a few can lead to extraordinary growth in the numbers of those who try to live out God's dream. 'The reign of

God is like this. A man takes a mustard seed, the smallest seed in the world, and plants it in the ground. After a while it grows up and becomes the biggest of all plants. It puts out such large branches that the birds of the air come and make their nests in its shade.'[13] These parables illustrate the small beginnings of the kingdom and its great future by using examples of extraordinary growth.

An interesting example of grace bringing God's reign to bear on the life of one individual is to be found in St Paul's account of his conversion. 'You have heard of my former way of life in Judaism, how I persecuted the church of God beyond measure and tried to destroy it, and progressed in Judaism beyond many of my contemporaries among my race, since I was even a zealot for my ancestral traditions. But God, who from my mother's womb had set me apart and *called me through his grace*, was pleased to reveal his Son to me, so that I might proclaim him to the Gentiles.'[14]

Jesus saw his ministry as God's battle with evil in all its forms: mutual fear, aggressive competitiveness, poverty, oppression, hunger, illness and even death. To the extent that evil, in any of its many forms, is overcome, God's reign exists. Wherever evil continues, the kingdom has still to come. Hence Jesus could say, 'The kingdom of God is among you,'[15] and yet ask us to pray, 'Thy Kingdom come.'

God's reign has to incorporate the poor and the powerless. 'Blessed are you poor, the kingdom of God is yours.'[16] The poor are blessed not because they live in poverty, which is an evil, but because they are open to God's dream that challenges the very cultural values and conditions that have made them poor and powerless in the first place. God's future reign gives them hope because they know that resurrection will dawn one day and they will reign with Jesus on the new earth that God, through human instrumentality, is now, often imperceptibly, building throughout history.

Jesus challenged the deep-seated human desires for

wealth, prestige and power over others because they get in the way of creating human brother/sisterhood. This is especially evident in his parables that contain frequent reversals of fortune. Those who worked only one hour received the same wages as those who worked all day. One should invite not only friends but also unknown strangers to a banquet. The hated Samaritan is the one who teaches love of neighbour. The prodigal is accepted as readily as the dutiful. These reversals challenge deeply held values and invite people to enter imaginatively into a different sort of world.

Jesus' sayings about money and possessions are among the hardest in the gospel. 'No one can serve two masters; for a slave will either hate one and love the other, or be devoted to one and despise the other. You cannot serve God and wealth.'[17] 'How hard it is for those who have wealth to enter the kingdom of God … It is easier for a camel to pass through the eye of a needle than for the one who is rich to enter the kingdom of God. (The disciples) were exceedingly astonished and said among themselves, "Then who can be saved?" Jesus looked at them and said, "For human beings it is impossible, but not for God. All things are possible for God.'[18] In other words, it would take a miracle to get the rich into the kingdom, to share God's vision for humanity. The miracle would consist in getting them to give up their wealth by sharing it with others.

The same theme is to be found in Jesus' parable of the Rich Man and Lazarus. 'There was a rich man who dressed in purple garments and fine linen and dined sumptuously each day. And lying at his door was a poor man named Lazarus, covered with sores, who would gladly have eaten his fill of the scraps that fell from the rich man's table. Dogs even came and licked his sores. When the poor man died, he was carried away by angels to the bosom of Abraham. The rich man also died and was buried, and from the netherworld, where he was in torment, he raised his eyes and saw Abraham far off and Lazarus at his side. And he cried out, "Father Abraham, have pity on me. Send Lazarus to dip the tip of his finger in water and cool my tongue, for I am suffering torment in these flames." Abraham replied, "My child, remember that you received what was good during your lifetime while Lazarus likewise received what was bad; but now he is comforted here, whereas you are tormented. Moreover, between us and you a great chasm is established to prevent anyone from crossing who might wish to go from our side to yours or from your side to ours." He said, "Then I beg you, send him to my father's house, for I have five brothers, so that he may warn them, lest they too come to this place of torment." But Abraham replied, "They have Moses and the prophets. Let them listen to them." He said "Oh no, father Abraham, but if someone from the dead goes to them, they will repent." Then Abraham said, "If they will not listen to Moses and the prophets, neither will they be persuaded if someone should rise from the dead."'[19]

The different fates of the rich man and Lazarus after death 'are not based on the rich man having lived a life of vice, and Lazarus having been virtuous. They are based on the rich man having had a comfortable and well-fed life, while Lazarus was hungry and miserable. This attack on the Pharisees' love of money is made all the sharper by the point made at the end of the parable. If they did not listen to Moses and the prophets, they will not listen to someone come back from the dead. To Luke's readers/hearers this would appear prophetic, for Acts will show that people did not listen even after Jesus came back from the dead.'[20]

Again Jesus was calling for a shift in attitude. Rather then hoarding selfishly and simply taking care of number one, one's family or even one's nation, Jesus demanded a sharing of resources so that the plight of 'widows, orphans and strangers', the outcasts of the world, are not ignored. In his parable of the Last Judgment Jesus even talks about *the nations of the world* being judged by the way they treat the poor and the oppressed.

Christians who are well off have often watered down Christ's teaching about money. They sometimes claim that they are 'spiritually poor'. The Bible does indeed equate the 'poor' with those who are humble or meek, but always in contrast to idolaters or blind rich people. The primary meaning of 'poor' refers to those who are economically poor. When the 'poor in spirit' are praised[21] it is because, in addition to their material poverty, they tend to be more open to God's presence and love. Spiritual poverty does not refer to wealthy individuals who are unhappy in the midst of their prosperity or are indifferent to their wealth. The 'poor in spirit' are almost without exception power-less, oppressed people who experience serious economic and social deprivation. Where such conditions exist, God's kingdom is 'not yet'. When the kingdom comes 'those who are last will be first, and those who are first will be last.'[22]

St Paul, in his first letter to Timothy, wrote: 'As for those in the present age who are rich, command them not to be haughty, or to set their hopes on the uncertainty of riches, but rather on God, who richly provides us with everything for our enjoyment. They are to do good, to be rich in good works, generous and ready to share, thus storing up for themselves the treasure of a good foundation for the fu-ture, so they may take hold of life that really is life.'[23]

Bonnie Thurston tells a story that is very much in the spirit of what St Paul had in mind. 'A very young family had struggled through the diagnosis of cancer with their small daughter. The child was about five years old and had endured many surgeries, many treatments, and chemotherapy that had left her bald. But her prognosis was good, and the family decided to go out to dinner to celebrate. They didn't choose an elegant restaurant, but they chose a good one. Of course, they were worried about how people might react to their active, cheerful, bald daughter. They thought a better class of people, nicer people, might be found in a better restaurant. You know, people less likely to stare. So they dressed up and went out for their party.

It was a good choice of restaurant, subdued, slightly darkened, and pleasant. The hostess didn't bat an eye as she seated the family. The waiter brought the menus, rattled off the specials and didn't stare. The family chose their dinners. The bread and salads appeared and then … yes, you guessed it, the little girl had to go to the restroom. Most of us have faced it, the long walk across the dining room with a child in tow. So the mother got up with the daughter. The very attractive, even elegant lady at the next table smiled kindly as they passed.

Off they went to the ladies' room, and they accomplished the business at hand. But as they were leaving the restroom, the lady from the next table came in. She knelt down by the little bald girl and said, "You've had cancer, haven't you?" "Oh, no," thought the little girl's mother, "now what?" and she prepared to go into her protective mode (you know it, mothers, the Protective Mode). But the elegant lady continued, "Me too. And I'm bald too." At which point she removed her hairdo and plopped it down on the little girl's head. The child was delighted. She raced to the full-length mirror as the two older women grinned and told her how lovely she looked. The women had a conversation about cancer and recovery while the little girl giggled delightedly and played with the wig. After a time, they all returned to their tables. The elegant lady winked at her escort and resumed her dinner.

But the little girl couldn't wait to tell her Dad what had happened and how grown up she looked in the wig. And before her mother could either explain or stop her, she had slipped off her chair, hopped over to the elegant lady's table and asked, "May I borrow your hair to show my Dad?"

Picture it now … The nice restaurant. The attractive

clientele. The elegant lady and her escort. "May I borrow your hair to show my Dad?" And as the little girl's horrified mother looked on, the elegant lady took off her lovely wig and placed it carefully on the little girl's head. "Go show your Daddy, sweetheart."'[24]

The elegant lady demonstrated costly generosity by not standing on her dignity or appealing to the status that comes from wealth, but rather, in St Paul's words, by being generous and ready to share in a way that gave life.

In the oriental world *status* is highly prized, even to the point where people will sometimes commit suicide rather than forfeit it. In Jesus' time status was also a dominant value. People lived off the respect that others gave them. Jesus contradicted this way of valuing people. He criticised the Scribes and Pharisees, for example, not because of their teaching but because of the way they lived for the prestige and admiration given to them by others. Speaking about them to his disciples, Jesus said, 'all their works are performed to be seen. They widen their phylacteries and lengthen their tassels. They love the places of honour at banquets, seats of honour in synagogues, greetings in marketplaces, and the salutation "Rabbi".'[25] Even religious practices such as prayer, fasting or almsgiving could be done simply *'so that people may see them'*. In God's kingdom status has no role to play. People are to be valued simply because they are sons and daughters of a loving God.

'Some will find it very difficult to imagine what such a life would be like but the "babes" who have never had any of the privileges of status and those who have not valued it will find it very easy to appreciate the fulfillment that life in such a society would bring. Those who could not bear to have beggars, former prostitutes, servants, women and children treated as their equals, who could not live without feeling superior to at least some people, would simply not be at home in God's kingdom as Jesus understood it. They would want to exclude themselves from it.'[26]

Jesus' attitude to power differed greatly from the way

we tend to look at it. We think of power in terms of over-
riding authority, domination and force. Power in God's
kingdom is the power of loving service. Jesus said, 'You
know that those who are recognised as rulers over the
Gentiles lord it over them, and their great ones make their
authority over them felt. But it shall not be so among you.
Rather, whoever wishes to be first among you will be the
slave of all. For the Son of Man did not come to be served
but to serve and to give his life as a ransom for many.'[27]
Service not domination is what is required of Jesus' followers, even to the point of giving one's life for others.

Jesus saw how many of the Jewish leaders used the law
to dominate and oppress their own people. The Scribes
and Pharisees, he said, 'tie up heavy burdens and lay them
on people's shoulders, but they will not lift a finger to
move them.'[28] Jesus was not opposed to the Law as such.
He was opposed to the way the Scribes and Pharisees
made the Law into a burden instead of a service. Jesus was
permissive whenever people's needs were not met by the
Law and strict whenever observance of the Law would
best meet their needs. 'As Jesus was passing through a
field of grain on the Sabbath, his disciples began to make a
path while picking the heads of grain. At this the Pharisees
said to him, "Look, why are they doing what is unlawful
on the Sabbath?" He said to them, "Have you never read
what David did when he was in need and he and his companions were hungry? How he went into the house of God
when Abiathar was high priest and ate the bread of offering that only the priests could lawfully eat, and shared it
with his companions?" Then he said to them, "The
Sabbath is made for man, not man for the Sabbath. That is
why the son of Man is lord even of the Sabbath".'[29] The
purpose of the Law, as Jesus saw it, was love, compassion
and service. The leaders in Jesus' time, however, used it to
enhance their own prestige and, by surrounding it with
petty regulations, used it to maintain their power over oth-

ers, something not unknown throughout history – even in the church!

Jesus not only proclaimed God's reign, God's dream for humanity, he demonstrated what it would look like in practice. He dined (had table-fellowship) with the religious outcasts of his day, with 'the rabble who knew nothing of the Law', as the Pharisees called them. 'While he was at table (in Levi's house), many tax collectors and sinners sat with Jesus and his disciples, for there were many who followed him. Some scribes who were Pharisees saw that he was eating with sinners and tax collectors and said to his disciples, "Why does he eat with tax collectors and sinners?" Jesus heard this and said to them, "Those who are well do not need a physician, but the sick do. I did not come to call the righteous but sinners".'[30] Jesus gave special importance to those people who were written off in social and religious terms and no longer counted in fashionable society. By sharing a meal with them, he demonstrated that they were important to God. Eating together has a religious significance, especially so in the East.

Jesus scandalised the people of his time by his easy approach to women. We find them accompanying him and providing for him and the Twelve as he journeyed from town to town. He even entered into a dialogue with a Samaritan woman although his fellow countrymen hated the Samaritans.[31] Mark mentions the 'women who had followed him when he was in Galilee and ministered to him. There were also many other women who had come up with him to Jerusalem.' As he hung on the cross 'there were many women there, looking on from a distance who had followed Jesus from Galilee, ministering to him.' In the eyes of his contemporaries such actions placed him in a state of religious impurity.

Jesus performed healing miracles that were more than kind deeds to help individuals. They also spoke of God's future triumph over all the powers of evil when the reign

of God was fully realised. They were signs and partial real-
isations of what was to happen in a yet-to-be realised future.
We will return to the question of miracles later on.

Jesus stressed the need to show mercy without measure, love without limits. He seemed to be calling us to rise
above the arena and atmosphere of blow and counter-
blow to the only level where justice is even remotely possible, the level of mercy and love. Otherwise we cut off the
possibility of reaching that place where we can respond to
one another with mutual respect, reconciliation, forgiveness, love and justice. Such virtue, however, is only possible for those who have experienced God's own gracious
self-giving, God's merciful forgiveness and unconditional
love and acceptance.

God's kingdom is not simply an individual, inner
experience but one that depends on and tends towards the
forming of community. There is a common mistranslation
of a saying of Jesus that reads 'The kingdom of God is
within you.' What Jesus actually said was 'The kingdom of
God is among you.' He demonstrated this by gathering
followers around him. They were to love one another,
share what they had, forgive one another and be willing, if
necessary, to die for the sake of God's kingdom where the
poor would no longer be poor, the hungry would be satis-
fied and the oppressed would be set free. Wherever this
occurred the kingdom of God was present.

The kingdom does not come into existence suddenly at
the end of time but is being created gradually over the
course of human history. Wherever people strive, with
God's grace, to build communities of truth, justice and
love, God's dream for humanity is taking shape. While it is
essentially God's project, human cooperation will determine the nature of the final outcome. Human beings,
under the guidance of God's Spirit, have to play their part
in building the 'new earth'. How exactly this renewed
earth will look, no one can say for 'eye has not seen, nor

ear heard, nor has it entered into the human mind what God has in store for those who love him.'[32]

What we call 'eternal life' will not be simply a reward to replace what we have done or suffered in this life. It will be a new construct, an absolutely new future, that will be radically different from the sort of time and space world we live in now: a world that is being brought to birth, slowly and often painfully, in and through the course of history. 'God will bring all creation together, everything in heaven and on earth.'[33]

Being in tune with God's dream, with God's kingdom, gives meaning to human existence and should be the driving force that urges Christians to action in the world. As Jesus put it, 'Strive first for the kingdom of God and his righteousness.'[34] To strive in this way means building the human community by 'reading the signs of the times', developing a critical awareness of the world and its injustices and doing what can be done, with God's grace, to overcome them. Today this means involving the poor themselves as well as politicians, economists, sociologists and all those who have the sort of expertise that can contribute to bettering the lot of humanity, particularly of those who are poor or marginalised in any way.

Seeking the kingdom also means seeing the seeds of the kingdom already present in the world: in the men and women who rear and educate families, who work for justice and peace, who seek to reconcile conflict, who care for the sick and work with the marginalised, who stand with the poor and the powerless. It is in this sense that the kingdom of God is among us. For those, however, who pursue wealth, prestige and power for their own sake, the kingdom will remain a secret, a mystery.

Using the cultural language of his time, Jesus also spoke of another type of kingdom, the kingdom of Satan. This kingdom is the very antithesis of God's dream for humanity because it leads to the breakdown of human relationships by promoting rugged individualism, greed and domination. Those who are so established in power, prestige and security that they refuse to gaze on their fellow human beings with compassion 'belong' to the kingdom of Satan. What is at stake here is power: the power of God's love on the one hand, the power of evil on the other. God's power is the power of love and compassion, truth, justice and freedom. Satan's power is seen in severed relationships, in lies, hatred, injustice, exploitation, poverty, oppression, tyranny and war.

Jesus' first words in the gospel of Mark were 'The kingdom of God is close at hand. Repent, and believe the Good News.' (1:13) Repentance means more than simply saying 'I am sorry.' It is a profound change in the way we behave so that, as followers of Christ, we open ourselves to others and especially the powerless in ways that are life-giving. It can be frightening to reach out to the poor and those on the margins of society. Those of us who are well off tend to develop our own language, mindset and ways of living that separate us from the two-thirds of suffering humanity.

Conversion means coming to see and treat others, especially those who suffer, as brothers and sisters. This is no easy task. People prefer to mix with their own kind and remain fearful of those who differ from them in language, religion, social class or colour. From childhood, people build their own 'maps' of the world, ways of seeing and understanding it and ways of relating to one another within it. Conditioned by family, friends, school, church and their social environment, such maps provide them with security and those who fall outside known boundaries are suspect. People are slow to change the way they view those who are different and fail to realise that there are other islands of knowledge, other ways of thinking, speaking about and experiencing the world, other equally valid cultures even within their own cities and towns.

Jesus maintained that to be a follower of his one had to

enlarge one's map of the world and, above all, see it from the perspective of the poor and the oppressed. When one comes to realise that all men and women are one's brothers and sisters, children of the same Father, one's heart is changed, one's perspective altered and a desire to do something about injustice is set alight.

To see life from the perspective of the poor can be challenging and even frightening and is one reason why 'conversion' can be such a slow process. To cross the divide, even the physical one, that separates the well off from the poor, can entail real sacrifice. When those on the other side of the tracks are regarded as enemies, such a crossing becomes all the more difficult. Jesus said, 'You have heard it said, "Love your friends, hate your enemies." But now I tell you: love your enemies and pray for those who persecute you, so that you may become the children of your father in heaven. For he makes his sun to shine on bad and good alike, and gives rain to those who do good and to those who do evil. Why should God reward you if you love only those who love you? Even the tax collectors do that! And if you speak only to your friends, have you done anything out of the ordinary? Even the pagans do that! You must be perfect – just as your father in heaven is perfect.'[35]

Jesus' words and actions brought him into conflict with the leaders of Judaism. His protest against the temple traders, his statements about the Law being at the service of human beings, his solidarity with those unversed in the Law, his mixing with the outcasts of society, his dealings with women, his criticisms and denunciations of the priestly caste, his calling God Father, made it inevitable that his enemies would try to silence him and bring about his death by crucifixion. 'The chief priests and scribes were seeking a way put him to death, yet they feared him because the whole crowd was astonished at his teaching.'[36]

However, political/religious expediency finally led to

Jesus' crucifixion. This proved a shattering blow to his followers. Discouraged by the arrest and crucifixion of Jesus,
the apostles fled Jerusalem and made their way back to
Galilee, their hopes dashed and their faith shattered.

Chapter 7

Resurrection

If Christ is proclaimed as raised from the dead, how can some of you say there is no resurrection of the dead? If there is no resurrection of the dead, then Christ has not been raised; and if Christ has not been raised, then our proclamation has been in vain and your faith has been in vain.[37]

Shortly after Jesus' death something very strange happened. The apostles experienced Jesus as alive! God's response to Jesus' faithfulness, his blazing honesty and love for humanity, was to raise him from death. Jesus no longer remained in the tomb or lay rotting in the ground. His tomb was found empty on Easter morning.[38]

While many Jews, in Jesus' time, believed in a general resurrection of the dead at the end of time, there was certainly no expectation of the resurrection of any particular man from the dead prior to that. Nor was resurrection of the dead a universally accepted notion. The Sadducees, for example, denied the resurrection of the dead while the Pharisees did accept the idea of a general resurrection.[39] Jesus would have seen himself as one who would be raised from the dead on the last day but it is unlikely that he foresaw his own individual resurrection. Where there are references in the gospel to Jesus foretelling his own resurrection, these were, in all probability, simply a reading back into his earthly life by the early church of what they knew about him in the light of his resurrection.

But, one may well ask, what did the apostles actually experience at the time of Jesus' resurrection? One of the

fascinating things we find, in reading the resurrection accounts in the New Testament, is that when Jesus appears
to his followers they do not recognise him at first. Two examples from the gospel of St Luke illustrate the point. As
two of the disciples were conversing and debating on the
road to Emmaus, 'Jesus himself drew near and walked
with them, but their eyes were prevented from recognising
him.'[40] Later Jesus appeared to the eleven apostles and
others. He 'stood in their midst and said to them "Peace be
with you." But they were startled and terrified and
thought that they were seeing a ghost.'[41] The reason for
such reactions is that, having died, Jesus had passed into a
transformed mode of existence, a new way of being, that is
beyond history, and certainly beyond the day to day
experience of the disciples, not to mention our own day to
day experience.

St Paul too claimed to have seen the risen Jesus.
However, he went on to say that Jesus' risen body was a
'spiritual' body by which he meant that it possessed very
different properties from those found in ordinary mortals.
The risen Christ had the ability to move through closed
doors, to move from one place to another with great rapid-
ity, to appear suddenly in unexpected places.[42] For Paul,
while the risen Christ was the same person who had
walked the roads of Israel and there was a clear continuity
with his former life, there was also a profound transformation in his mode of existence.

It is important not to be overly literal in trying to understand what really happened to Paul and the apostles. Their
experience of the risen Christ was unlike any other experience. They were dealing with someone who had passed
beyond the boundaries of space and time and yet remained intimately present to them. They continued to experience, or began to experience, in one way or another,
the power of Jesus' presence among them after his death.

While one has to keep in mind the tendency to embroider

particular incidents as they are told and retold, whatever the actual nature of the 'appearances' of Jesus they were clearly experiences that transformed the lives of his followers. Even if at first they doubted (Matthew 28:17), did not believe that he had risen (Mark 16:11-12), did not recognise him (John 20:14), and even wanted proof that he was alive (John 20:25), they soon began to experience Jesus as alive and present to them in a new way.

Some of course have argued that what the disciples meant by Jesus' resurrection was a purely subjective experience implying that the cause that Jesus stood for was still valid in spite of his death. Others have argued that Jesus' life and teaching so inspired the apostles that they made up the resurrection stories to affirm his continuing influence in their lives. However, it is hardly credible that subjective experiences alone could suddenly produce such a profound and radical change in men and women who had fearfully returned to their former lives after Jesus' death. Jesus' appearances radically changed the lives of his followers. They gave them courage, in spite of much adversity, to announce to the world that Jesus had indeed risen and then set out to spread his teaching, even to the point of laying down their lives for the gospel.

However, we have to ask whether the idea of someone rising from the dead is compatible with modern scientific thought. John Polkinghorne, a former Cambridge Professor of Mathematical Physics, has this to say about the idea of resurrection: 'Clearly such an idea (resurrection) goes beyond our direct experience but it seems to me in no way to run counter to it. There is nothing particularly important in the actual physical constituents of our bodies. After a few years nutrition and wear and tare the atoms that make us up have nearly all been replaced by equivalent successors. It is the pattern they form which constitutes the physical expression of our continuing personality. There seems no difficulty in conceiving of that pattern, dissolved in death, being recreated in another environment. In terms of a crude analogy it would be like transforming the software of a computer programme (the 'pattern' of our personality) from one piece of hardware (our body in the world) to another (our body in the world to come.) Scientifically this seems a coherent idea.'[43]

More than any other scientist, Wernher Von Braun was responsible for putting Americans on the moon. Before he died, he gave this testimony concerning life after death: 'I think science has a real surprise for the skeptics … Nothing in nature, not even the tiniest particle, can disappear without trace. Nature does not know extinction. All it knows is transformation … Everything science has taught me – and continues to teach me – strengthens my belief in the continuity of our spiritual existence after death.'[44]

But even if life after death may be considered a scientifically coherent idea, what significance, if any, does Jesus' resurrection have for those of us who live in the twenty-first century? There are two levels on which to answer this question, the personal and the communal. On a personal level, the greatest fear that most human beings have to face is probably the fear of death. To be human is to die. Death can haunt us like nothing else because we fear annihilation, the loss of self and the loss of our most significant relationships. Either we die into nothingness or we die into the mysterious, incomprehensible reality we call God. The good news of Christianity is that for those who die life is changed not ended. 'Since we believe that Jesus died and rose again, even so, through Jesus, God will bring with him those who have died.'[45]

Imagine for a moment if you could talk to a baby in the womb and explain how the cord that unites it to its mother gives it life. Then if you were to tell the baby that it was going to be expelled from the womb, that the umbilical cord was going to be cut and that it would be pushed through a narrow passage into a very different world, the baby might well fear that it was going to die. Being born would seem like death.

Death is a kind of rebirth leading to resurrection. We cling tenaciously to the cord of life but eventually we must let go before entering a new world without shadow, darkness, loneliness, suffering, isolation or pain. We return to the God from whom we come and to whom we go, to a world where all the longings of the human heart at last find fulfilment. Our difficulty with death is that we are only able to see it from one side. Those who have died do not return to tell us what lies beyond. While we have no direct experience of resurrection, there are human analogies which may give us a glimpse of what it might look like: the joy of reunion with loved ones after a very long separation; new beginnings in a relationship after extreme failure and disappointment; feeling alive again after coming to terms with serious illnesses or some addiction; experiencing freedom from an oppressive regime, not to mention the 'dyings and risings' we see in nature – these are all types of 'resurrection'.

Some years ago, after suffering a serious heart attack, I went through a period of mild depression, a sort of mini death. Immediately after that experience, thoughts of possible death were very much on my mind. In the immediate aftermath, when I was on my own, I sometimes cried quietly, just feeing sorry for myself I suppose! But gradually through the help of very close friends, of prayer, family and the encouragement of my cardiologist, the depression lifted. I began to discover that, in spite of the daily tablet taking, having to avoid certain foods, being unable to climb stairs and do all the sort of things that come easily to a relatively young man, life was indeed worth living. The sun came out again. A little 'resurrection' had happened. Was it a foretaste of things to come? It seems that to experience the joy of any 'resurrection' we have to accept the reality of what precedes it, namely a 'death' of some kind.

But there is another aspect of resurrection that we must consider. Jesus addressed his message not simply to individuals but to the whole Israelite community and indeed to all the nations of the world. Christ tells us that there will be a future judgment of the nations. 'When the Son of Man comes, *all the nations of the earth* will be gathered before him, and he will separate people one from another as a shepherd separates the sheep from the goats.' Those nations that feed the hungry, assuage thirst, welcome strangers, clothe the naked and take care of the sick will be welcomed into the fullness of God's kingdom while those that do not can have no part in it.[46]

'Lord, you know well that today there are not only rich and poor individuals. There are rich, even excessively rich, countries and there are poor countries. You know, too, that the difference is becoming even greater rather than less. Help men and women of good will – from every land and colour and language and religion – to bring liberating moral pressure to bear on authorities and awaken their consciences so that all will help the human race to be freed from the shame of the subhuman beings whom wretchedness produces, and from the shame of the superhuman who are begotten of excessive prosperity and luxury. Help those who have the happiness of being born in rich countries; help them to see that the privileges they enjoy have been bought by injustice to the poor countries. Without realising it, they often become accomplices of this injustice ... Money, power, fame, middle-class complacency breed selfishness. Selfishness is the beast that lurks within us, swallows us up and leads us to swallow others up. Help your human creatures to flee false riches and plunge into the riches for which all of us were born: the one undivided love, love of God and love of humankind.'[47]

Those peoples and nations that suffer grievous injustices must find redress, if not in this world then in the world to come. God's justice must not only be done but be seen to be done. However, because 'Christ has been raised from the dead, *the first fruits of those who have died,*'[48] the oppressed can look forward to a radically new future – God's fully realised kingdom where all human history and culture, all the suffering that human beings have had to endure, are to be transfigured in a redeemed world of relationships that exceed by far our wildest dreams of knowing and being known, of loving and being loved. Scripture can only hint at what that future will look like using analogies to describe what 'no eye has seen, nor ear heard, nor the human heart conceived, what God has prepared for those who love him'.[49] It speaks of a banquet, a wedding feast, an eternal city, paradise.

'We do not know the moment of the consummation of the earth and of humanity nor the way the universe will be transformed. The form of this world, distorted by sin, is passing away and we are taught that God is preparing a new dwelling and a new earth in which righteousness dwells, whose happiness will fill and surpass all the desires of peace arising in human hearts ... We have been warned, of course, that it profits us nothing if we gain the whole world and lose or forfeit ourselves. Far from diminishing our concern to develop this earth, the expectation of a new earth should spur us on, for it is here that the body of a new human family grows, foreshadowing in some way the age which is to come. That is why, although we must be careful to distinguish earthly progress clearly from the increase of the kingdom of Christ, such progress is of vital concern to the kingdom of God, insofar as it can contribute to the better ordering of human society.'[50]

Men and women of good faith have to work with God to build a radical future, one that is powerfully subversive because it questions all present social, political and economic structures that so often are the cause of human suffering. Because Christians are called on to co-create anticipations of God's reign in history, there is real urgency to their engagement in this world at all levels, including socio-economic and political levels.

'When we have spread on earth the fruits of our nature and our enterprise – human dignity, sisterly and brotherly communion, and freedom – according to the command of the Lord and in his Spirit, we will find them once again, cleansed this time from the stain of sin, illuminated and transfigured, when Christ presents to his Father an eternal and universal kingdom of truth and life, a kingdom of holiness and grace, a kingdom of justice, love and peace. Here on earth the kingdom is mysteriously present; when the Lord comes it will enter into its perfection.'[51]

Jesus said to his disciples, 'Do not let your hearts be troubled. Believe in God and believe also in me. In my Father's house there are many dwelling places. If it were not so, would I have told you that I go to prepare a place for you? And if I go and prepare a place for you, I will come again and will take you to myself, so that where I am, there you may be also.'[52] Herein lies the hope that enables suffering humanity to face life with all its complexities, to struggle against its evils and face even death itself – with confidence.

Either we take Jesus at his word or we don't. Those who work and wait for 'new heavens and a new earth, where righteousness is at home,'[53] believe that God 'will wipe away every tear; death will be no more; mourning and crying and pain will be no more' and there will be 'a new heaven and a new earth.'[54] Resurrection will have dawned.

CHAPTER 8

Jesus as Saviour

What do we mean when we say that Jesus was the saviour of the world? Theologians, using terms like atonement, reparation, satisfaction and expiation, have tried, over the centuries, to explain the meaning of the salvation won for us by Jesus. But 'it may be well to clear away one common and deadly piece of nonsense. Making "atonement", offering "reparation", performing some work of "satisfaction", "expiating sin" or whatever similar term we wish to use, does *not* coincide with "propitiating" an angry God bent on "punishing" his Son for the sins of the human race.'[55] The constant danger with such language is that it appears to imply that Jesus was made a scapegoat for the evils of the world in order to appease an angry God. Nothing could be further from the truth.

One thing is very clear from the gospels: Jesus did not seek his own death. He even prayed to be delivered from it.[56] However if his words, actions and the kingdom values that he stood for were to lead to his death, he was prepared to accept the inevitable. God's message of love, reconciliation and liberation meant more to him than his own life.

Perhaps Jesus saw his parable of the tenants as a foreshadowing of his own fate. 'There was a landowner (God) who planted a vineyard (Israel), put a hedge around it, dug a winepress in it, and built a tower. Then he leased it to tenants (Israel's leaders) and went on a journey. When vintage time came near, he sent his servants (the prophets) to obtain his produce. But the tenants seized the servants and one they beat, another they killed, and a third they stoned. Again he sent other servants, more numerous than the first ones, but they treated them in the same way. Finally he sent his son (Jesus) to them, thinking "They will respect my son.' But when the tenants saw the son, they said to one another, "This is the heir. Come let us kill him and acquire his inheritance. They seized him, threw him out of the vineyard and killed him".'[57]

God did not set out to punish Jesus for the sins of humanity. Such an idea runs contrary to the way Jesus perceived his Father, whom he called, in very intimate language, Abba, dear Father! A loving father, venting his anger on his son, would hardly have said of him 'This is my beloved son with whom I am well pleased.'[58] To press a very inadequate analogy, Jesus' Father is like a man who sees his son going off to a distant land, working to recon-cile those who were estranged and bring justice to the oppressed. The father knows that what his son is under-taking is dangerous and could well lead to his death but, with a heavy heart, out of love for those who suffer, he ap-proves his son's mission. In somewhat similar fashion, 'God so loved the world that he sent his only son', thereby demonstrating God's boundless love for humanity, espe-cially for the weak and the wounded.

If Jesus was not seeking to placate an angry Father, how was his death by crucifixion a source of salvation for men and women today? Mary Grey offers a valuable insight. 'In the birthing experience we (women) are given a "let-ting go" of self – in pain and struggle – for the creation of new being. We are given the sense of our physical bodies falling or even being torn apart. We have lost our "centred self". Nobody can reach us in this struggle, neither hus-band, lover, nor parent. We are in the dark, alone, in that primeval womb of chaos from which all life emerged. And yet, in that very darkness we can meet God as creative cen-tre. We are held by that nurturing centre: from this being torn-apart, this sense of loss, together You and I wordlessly create new life.'[59]

Jesus, in the darkness of his suffering, death and seeming abandonment, entrusted himself entirely to the Father and out of that act of faith a new birthing was made possible because, as John's gospel tells us, Jesus 'handed over his Spirit', which is to say he not only breathed his last but, in that same breath, handed over his Spirit to the believing community.[60] Possessing Jesus' Spirit would enable his followers not only to experience something that was unheard of before in human history, someone rising from the dead, but also to discover a new way to salvation.

'Salvation' means more than simply 'saving one's soul'. Salvation is deliverance from evil of any sort including deliverance from the dangers that prevent people from reaching their final destiny – union with God in love. People are to be saved from all types of suffering not merely personal guilt. Whenever people suffer, either individually or collectively, there is need for salvation not just in the next life but in this one as well. Those who suffer exploitation, the very poor, the unemployed, the addicted, asylum seekers, victims of war, the starving millions, should not be asked to wait for 'pie-in-the-sky when they die'. Jesus' Good News is a call to save such people from their suffering in the here and now while, at the same time, pointing to a future when 'the little ones of the earth', those who have been cast aside, the poor, the hungry, those who mourn, the hated, will be rewarded with the fullness of eternal life for what they have had to endure in this present life.

The early Christians experienced the power of Jesus' presence among them and were convinced that he was still guiding and inspiring them through the power of the Spirit he had promised them. 'I will ask the Father, and he will give you another advocate to be with you always. The advocate will teach you everything and remind you of all that I told you.'[61] God's Spirit cannot be separated from God. It is not some magical substance separate from God but is God near to, within, inspiring, guiding the Christian community by teaching men and women of all generations the implications of who Jesus is and what he said and did.

Jesus, risen from the dead, is taken into God's mode of existence and activity. St Paul calls the risen Jesus 'a life-giving Spirit', 'the Lord who is Spirit', or talks about the 'Spirit of Jesus Christ'.[62] Through his Spirit, Jesus continues to be with his people whether at worship, or when helping, encouraging or comforting human beings, especially those pushed to the margins. Nor is the work of the Spirit confined to Christians. 'The wind blows where it wills, and you can hear the sound it makes, but you do not know where it comes from or where it goes; so it is with everyone who is born of the Spirit.'[63] 'Since Christ died for everyone, and since all are in fact called to one and the same destiny, which is divine, we must hold that the holy Spirit offers to all the possibility of being made partners, in a way known to God, in the paschal mystery.'[64]

How is the Spirit of Christ experienced today? As Mary Grey puts it, 'through the passionate breakthrough we call resurrection, relational energy was released for those open to it.' Christ's Spirit is active whenever people feeling depressed or terrified still find the strength to go on without knowing where that strength comes from. The Spirit is at work whenever people meet those who care profligately for others and wonder where that love comes from. The Spirit is moving the human heart when really poor or suffering people have a light in their eyes that does not square with their situation. When there is real care and love between people who should by all sociological and political accounts be at one another's throats – a poor black and a wealthy white South African, a Jew and an Arab, an Irish republican and a hard line unionist – the Spirit of Jesus is at work. When people experience the power of hatred, greed, prejudice and violence, and wonder how they are held in check, God's Spirit is at work. Perhaps in any or all such occurrences, people experience the light that the darkness cannot overcome because the Spirit of Jesus, the Life-Breath of God, has been poured into human hearts.

The cross of Jesus was a life-affirming protest against all human crucifixions and, at the same time, a call to action to rid the world of pain and suffering through healing, forgiveness and reconciliation. God, in Jesus, cries out against all forms of inhumanity and the cross of Jesus summons his followers to be co-creators, co-sufferers and co-redeemers through the power of God's self-giving in Christ.

'Human suffering, a suffering which impels us to action, can only be tolerated if Jesus' way of reconciliation, which revealed its radical character on Good Friday, becomes *a living remembrance* among us. As long as human beings try to use one another, the word God can only be used validly from a Christian point of view in criticism of those conditions which dishonour people, criticism which is backed up by appropriate action.'[65]

We know only too well that the realisation of God's dream for the world will meet with stiff opposition. Greed for money, power, status and domination, prevent human reconciliation. While reconciliation may flame out here and there for short periods of time in human history, the living remembrance of Jesus crucified and risen is a constant reminder that, in spite of apparent failure, love, which often seems useless and doomed to failure, can never acknowledge defeat. God's dream calls for a constant renewal of love that excludes no one and embraces, in a special way, all those on the margins.

Jesus' first followers came to recognise that what mattered was neither success nor failure as the world thinks of them. Human life, with its joys and sorrows, its sufferings, its compassionate love and concern for others, especially those who have been written off in the course of history, does have a future.

In spite of all our efforts we know that some day 'the heavens will be dissolved in flames and the elements melted in fire'.[66] However the ultimate fulfilment of the Creator's purpose will take place 'beyond' our present history. St Paul tells us that 'God raised the Lord and will also raise us by his power.'[67] For many, of course, belief in life eternal seems something incredible. However, in Jesus the Christ 'we are promised a good future, even for those who in and of themselves have no prospect of a future, those who are written off, chewed up in and through our history, even to the point of death.'[68]

What we call 'eternal life' is not simply a reward for what we have suffered in this life. Rather all human history and culture, even our sufferings, will be transfigured in ways we cannot foretell. 'Eye has not seen, nor ear heard, nor has it entered the human heart, what God has prepared for those who love him.'[69] The New Testament authors can only hint at what that future will hold. They speak of future joys in terms of an eternal banquet, a wedding feast or paradise. But even if the future is radically different from the joys and sorrows, the struggles and achievements of the here and now, there will be a recognisable continuity as well since all creation, all human history and culture, will be present in a transfigured way – even our sufferings will perhaps remain but now as redeemed memories, like Christ's wounds, revealing the joyous side of love. In the Spirit we will be invited to enter a world beyond the present, but embracing this present one, where we will participate in relationships which exceed by far the wildest dreams we have of knowing and being known, of loving and being loved. Humanity hopes for a fullness of life centred on its relationship with God and through this with everyone and everything else. Such is the salvation promised us by Jesus of Nazareth.

CHAPTER 9

Is Jesus the only Saviour?

Is Jesus' role as saviour unique? What about other religious traditions such as Islam, Buddhism, Hinduism and Judaism in which the Christian tradition is so deeply rooted: do they not also lead to union with God? Vatican Council II spoke about these other religions.

Speaking about the religion of Israel, 'the church of Christ acknowledges that in God's plan of salvation the beginnings of its faith and election are to be found in the patriarchs, Moses and the prophets. It professes that all Christ's faithful, who as people of faith are daughters and sons of Abraham (see Galatians 3:7), are included in the same patriarch's call and that the salvation of the church (God's people) is mystically prefigured in the exodus of God's chosen people from the land of bondage. On this account the church cannot forget that it received the revelation of the Old Testament by way of that people with whom God in his inexpressible mercy established the covenant.'[70]

'In Hinduism people explore the divine mystery and express it both in the limitless riches of myth and the accurately defined insights of philosophy. They seek release from the trials of the present life by ascetical practices, profound meditation and recourse to God in confidence and love.

'Buddhism in its various forms testifies to the essential inadequacy of this changing world. It proposes a way of life by which people can, with confidence and trust, attain a state of perfect liberation and reach supreme illumination either through their own efforts or with divine help.

'Muslims worship God, who is one, living and subsistent, merciful and almighty, the Creator of heaven and earth, who has spoken to humanity. They endeavor to submit themselves without reserve to the hidden decrees of God, just as Abraham submitted himself to God's plan, to whose faith Muslims eagerly link their own. Although not acknowledging him as God, they venerate Jesus as a prophet; his virgin mother they also honour, and even at times devoutly invoke. Further, they await the day of judgement and the reward of God following the resurrection of the dead. For this reason they highly esteem an upright life and worship God, especially by way of prayer, alms-deed and fasting.

'The Church rejects nothing of what is true and holy in these religions. It has a high regard for the manner of life and conduct, the precepts and doctrines which, although differing in many ways from its own teaching, nevertheless often reflect a ray of that truth which enlightens all men and women.'[71]

So the church seeks to enter into genuine dialogue with all those who seek answers to the mysteries of life: 'What is the meaning and purpose of life? Where does suffering originate, and what end does it serve? What is the ultimate mystery, beyond human explanation, which embraces our entire existence, from which we take our origin and towards which we tend.'[72]

Christians, of course, believe, that Christ is *the* way, the truth and the life that most assuredly leads us to union with God. (John 14:6) 'In him, in whom God reconciled all things to himself (see 2 Corinthians 5:18-19), people find the fullness of their religious life.'[73] The Acts of the Apostles makes the same point when Peter is quoted as saying, 'There is salvation in no one else, for there is no other name under heaven given among mortals by which we must be saved.' (Acts 4:12) St Paul says, 'There is one God; there is also one mediator between God and humankind, Christ Jesus, himself human, who gave himself as a ransom for all.' (1 Timothy 2:5-6)

But, if other religions can lead one to God, why claim that Christ has a unique position as *the* saviour of the world? Because, Christians believe, Jesus is divine, the fullest expression of God, 'the reflection of God's glory and the exact imprint of God's very being', so being united with him in faith, hope and love unites us to God in a unique way. The good news of the resurrection means that true Christians simply cannot keep silent. 'If Jesus is divine, then communion with Jesus, union with him in love, makes us divine by participation. If no other human being is divine as Jesus is, as the enfleshment of the Word of God, then the communion we can have with any other human being, what we can become through loving participation, is not divinity of the same sort, to the same degree, with the same implications for salvation (rescue from sin, establishment in wholeness), that communion with Jesus, through faith and hope and love inspired by the Spirit of Jesus, entails ... Despite rejection, abuse, terrible suffering, Jesus continued to trust his heavenly Father. The implications of what Jesus was (such a truster, such a believer) and how Jesus lived (with blazing honesty and love), apply always and everywhere as a revelation applicable universally. Nowhere else do I see enfleshed, incarnated, sacramentalised so clearly or deeply the faith, hope, and love that make the future absolutely good, trustworthy, for-us.'[74] One cannot but proclaim this from the housetops.

People are saved not by the words they use, the ideas they may have or even the orthodoxy they do or do not profess. People are saved by love and love alone – love of God, love of Jesus Christ and love shown to their fellow human beings. Love not only draws us into the mystery of God but also turns us towards our fellow human beings, especially the poorest and weakest. Love also turns us towards those of all other religions and of none since God 'wills everyone to be saved'.[75]

All human beings have been created in the image of God, which means that all have been endowed with Divine Power, with the potential to live out their lives in the love of God and share their love with their brothers and sisters, especially the most vulnerable. When they do so, then they are living as the gospel would want them to live, even if they are unaware of the fact that Jesus was the prefect expression of that love in the first place. 'God is love, and those who abide in love abide in God, and God abides in them' the first letter of John reminds us. (4:16) If men and women, of all religions or none, try to live lives of love, in conscious or unconscious imitation of Jesus, then they will find salvation, they will find God, or more precisely, God will find them and they will become one with him.

But while everyone may be endowed with the potential for self-giving love, especially for those on the margins, this is not the way many people choose to live their lives. They are profoundly influenced by the current climate with its competitive individualism, consumerism, possessiveness and money as the measure of everything that are regarded as *the* values to be pursued. Society encourages people to see themselves as having a right to total freedom in all things where the first and often the only duty is to oneself. In such a society self-giving, mutual love is devalued because it always involves a struggle to go beyond one's own selfish interests and look primarily to the well being of others. The primary role of the church, and of each Christian community, on the other hand is to make God's love, as expressed most perfectly in the life, death and resurrection of Jesus, a *conscious* and present reality in the world. 'By this everyone will know that you are my disciples, if you have love for one another.'[76]

If everyone, irrespective of one's religious allegiance, can be saved why bother to speak of Christ at all? Simply because those who have encountered Jesus, and formed themselves into a community of his disciples, always wish to share their story with others in the belief that Jesus, risen from death, is the one who reveals God and God's intentions most perfectly and because, by being united with Jesus, they can be led to God in a unique way. The good news of the resurrection gives wings to the feet – and voice to the tongue! True Christians cannot keep silent – even the soldiers at the tomb are depicted as having to be paid to keep quiet.[77] Christians share the good news about the resurrection because they cannot bottle it up, not because they don't respect others' beliefs or believe that other people cannot be saved. Sharing one's story never denigrates others' beliefs. Christians should not preach *at* those of other faiths, still less forcibly try to 'convert' them. We cannot truly pray to God the Father of all if we treat people as other than sisters or brothers, for all are created in God's image. People's relation to God and their relation to each other are so interdependent that scripture says, 'Whoever does not love does not know God, for God is love.'[78]

It is an interesting fact that Jesus did not try to 'convert' people. When Jesus healed the Roman centurion's servant, for example, he made no demand that he embrace Judaism. He simply commended him for his faith. 'I tell you, not even in Israel have I found such faith.[79] When relating the parable of the Good Samaritan to a lawyer, he did not say that the Samaritan should have become a disciple of Jesus.[80] Jesus did not try to convert the Gentile Syrophoenician woman but simply told her that her daughter would be cured.[81]

Jesus entered into dialogue with people of other faiths. He reached out to the mystery of God active in their lives. He was never coercive: nor should we be. The Spirit acts where it wills, so we should 'enter with prudence and charity into discussion and collaboration with members of other religions. Let Christians, *while witnessing to their own faith and way of life*, acknowledge, preserve and encourage the spiritual and moral truths found among non-Christians, together with their social life and culture.'[82]

Christians are called upon to tell the story of their encounter with God in and through Christ in the hope that, if others are interested enough, they too may wish to 'come and see' this Jesus who claimed to be 'the way, the truth and the life'. But even if they are not, as John Paul II has said, 'Christians will join hands with all men and women of goodwill and work together in order to bring about a more just and peaceful society in which the poor will be the first to be served.'[83] Nothing could be closer to the heart of Christ.

CHAPTER 10

Whatever happened to Hell?

We do not hear a lot about hell these days. It seems a long time ago since sermons on hellfire and brimstone were the order of the day. So, one asks, whatever happened to hell? Has it ceased to exist, like limbo? Does it make any sense to talk about it today? Where did the Jewish and Christian notion of hell come from?

There was a valley just outside Jerusalem called Gehenna. It was the place where, centuries before Christ, pagan gods were worshipped and children were burned alive as human sacrifices to the pagan god Molech. By the time of Jesus, the place was used as the Jerusalem rubbish dump where decomposing matter was eaten by worms and there was a continuously smoldering fire. Sometimes the bodies of plague victims were destroyed there. In Gehenna the worms never died and the fire was perpetually smoldering: everything and everyone else died, decomposed and was destroyed. In time Gehenna became the Jewish and Christian symbol of hell, of what it means to be eternally separated from God.

Jesus the Jew, a man of his time and culture, used this traditional Jewish imagery. 'If your eye causes you to sin, pluck it out. Better for you to enter into the kingdom of God with one eye than with two eyes to be thrown into Gehenna, where their worm does not die, and the fire is not quenched.'[84] When Jesus spoke about Gehenna, he was using a graphic metaphor to point out that when we freely, decisively and fundamentally refuse to love God and our neighbour, there are eternal consequences. When

people use their freedom to abuse their fellow human beings, to destroy their lives or marginalise them in any way,
they are cutting themselves off from God and, unless they
have a change of heart and behaviour (or what the Bible
calls 'conversion') they cannot be at one with God.

The call of the gospel is to love God and one's neighbour, even one's enemies. When people put wealth, status,
ancestry, education, power or other achievements before
love of God and one's fellow human beings, especially the
poorest and weakest, they are, in effect, cutting themselves
off from God. As the first letter of John pointed out,
'Whoever does not love does not know God, for God is
love ... No one has ever seen God; if we love one another,
God lives in us, and his love is brought to perfection in us
... Those who say, "I love God" and hate their brothers and
sisters, are liars; for those who do not love a brother or sis-
ter whom they have seen, cannot love God whom they
have not seen.'[85] To live without loving or being loved, to
live with hatred of self or others is to live in a sort of hell.
To live deliberately without loving others is to separate
oneself from God. To 'know' God, in the biblical sense, is
to be one with him. Only lovers can know God and be
united with him.

Hell is the destruction of one's spirit, of one's whole
personality, because it has become so absorbed and turned
in on itself, seeking only its own advantage, that it can no
longer relate to others and to God in life-giving ways and
so remains separate from God. What form such a separation might take we simply do not know, any more than
we know what heaven will be like.

But we can have some sense of what hell might mean if
we look at the pain and suffering of those who become estranged from each other in anger, or the pain and humiliation suffered by those who are violently abused, or the hell
on earth that the Jews had to endure during the Holocaust,
or the horrors of the killing fields that people had to en-

dure in Cambodia or Rwanda, or the sufferings and misery of the millions who starve daily in our world. Such people do suffer 'hell on earth'.

God envisages a future society (his kingdom) in which there will be no suffering and pain, no famine and plenty, no prestige and no status, no division of people into inferior and superior. All will be loved and respected, not because of their education or wealth or ancestry or power or status or virtue or other achievements, but simply because they are human beings, sons and daughters of God. In our dog-eat-dog world it may seem naïve to believe that all men and women will one day become brothers and sisters. The only possible answer is the one given by Jesus. 'For human beings it is impossible, but not for God. All things are possible for God.'[86] It is through our God-given love of our fellow human beings that God's dream will be gradually realised in human history and the power of evil will finally be overcome.

However, those who refuse to see beggars, former prostitutes, the oppressed, people of different nations, classes, colours and creeds as their brothers and sisters, will not be able to bear having such people treated as their equals. Because they cannot live without feeling superior to at least some people, they will simply not be at home in God's presence and will want to exclude themselves from it.

Is any human being in hell, eternally separated from God? We simply do not know. 'God predestines no one to go to hell: for this, a willful turning away from God is necessary, and persistence in it until the end.'[87] Since God 'wills everyone to be saved and to come to the knowledge of the truth',[88] it is right that we should hope that everyone will be saved and that, without understanding how this can be so, and without interfering with human freedom, all will in the end be prepared to say 'yes' to God's love. Perhaps, after death, those who have refused love may sit down at table with their enemies and undergo some sort of purification, some sort of purgatorial experience that will allow them to live in God's presence.

We cannot be united with God unless we freely choose to love him. Nor can we be united with God unless we love others. 'Whoever does not love remains in death. Everyone who hates his brother is a murderer, and you know that no murderer has eternal life remaining in him.'[89] To be in hell is to live without love in such a way that God, who always respects human freedom, is unable to fulfill all the longings of the human heart. The church's teaching about hell is essentially about taking human freedom seriously: it is a call to use that freedom responsibly by loving one's neighbour and refusing to do anything that would make life hell on earth for others. Jesus, in speaking about hell, was stressing that the refusal to love *does have eternal consequences.*

CHAPTER 11

Miracles

God's 'thoughts are not our thoughts, and his ways are not our ways,'[90] so when we pray for miracles, or for anything else for that matter, does God answer us? Is it reasonable today to believe in miracles?

If one has faith in God, it is hard to believe that he would not involve himself in the lives of human beings even if only as a persuading, sustaining and transforming presence. Christians believe that God does influence the conscious and unconscious minds of men and women without necessarily breaking any of the laws of nature. This gives God great leeway in his dealings with humanity. Nothing in science indicates incontrovertibly that God is tinkering with the laws of nature if he makes his presence felt in visions and dreams or if he communicates with us by answering prayers or offering guidance in the form of thoughts and inspirations.

While it is one thing to pray for inspiration and guidance, for courage and strength for oneself or others, it is quite a different matter to pray for rain or that someone should be cured of an inoperable cancer. We may make such prayers but, like Jesus, add the get-out clause 'yet not what I will but as you will.'[91] This may be because we recognise that what we want may not in fact be in our own best interest or what we want may clash with others' interests. While the farmer may pray for rain after a period of drought, I may want fine days for my holidays! Even when it comes to praying for someone with cancer, it may well be that death is the spiritual path that is in the person's best interest. Of course we cannot rule out the possibility that God, again without breaking the laws of nature, could influence the human psyche in such a way as to bring about physical healing. 'The extent to which physical healing is connected with the mind is too poorly understood for us to rule out its taking place as a result of God's activity in our minds.'[92]

Miracles happen around us all the time. Creation is a miracle; the growth of a tree from a tiny seed is a miracle; the birth of baby is a miracle. However, miracles that seem to sidestep the laws of nature, such as the dead coming back to life, strain the credulity of people in the twenty-first century.

The laws of nature govern how things change and adapt and, by implication, how things are not allowed to change. Although things do change over time, the basic underlying laws apparently do not. Having said that, the laws of nature are working scientific hypotheses that have to be reviewed and revised in the light of new evidence. Sometimes what we think of as a fundamental law of nature turns out to be merely an approximation, forcing scientists to search more deeply for the bedrock where laws never break down. No scientist pretends that to date that bedrock has been fully uncovered. Some scientists will tell you that even the latest scientific theory is not the last word about what is or is not possible in life and that even alleged miracles cannot be ruled out *a priori.*

Sir George Stokes, an eminent nineteenth-century physicist, once said: 'Admit the existence of a God, of a personal God, and the possibility of the miraculous follows at once. If the laws of nature are carried on in accordance with his will, he who willed them may will their suspension.' Granted that, what are we to make of the miracle stories found in the gospels?

Christians are not committed to *literally* believing every event dubbed miraculous as recorded in the Bible. Two examples, one Jewish , the other Christian, illustrate the point. The first is taken from the book of Joshua. 'On the day when the Lord gave the Amorites over to the Israelites, Joshua spoke to the Lord; and he said in the sight of Israel, "Sun, stand still at Gibeon, and Moon, in the valley of Aijalon." And the sun stood still, and the moon stopped until the nation took vengeance on their enemies. Is this not written in the Book of Jashar? The sun stopped in mid heaven, and did not hurry to set for about a whole day. There has been no day like it before or since, when the Lord heeded a human voice; for the Lord fought for Israel.'[93] If this were a literal, rather than an imaginative, poetic account of what happened when the Israelites were fighting the Amorites, we would have to ask not about what happened but about the things that did not happen. Why were there no major catastrophic climate disturbances, no enormous destructive tides, no gravitational consequences for the earth, the moon, or the remainder of the solar system? If the planets stopped in their tracks, why did they not plunge into the sun? The essence of the Joshua story, however, is simply that 'the Lord heeded a human voice', listened to a heartfelt prayer, and helped the Israelites in their victory over the Amorites. Talk about the sun standing still is simply epic accretion.

Another implausible story, this time from the gospels, is the story of the coin in the fish's mouth. 'When they reached Capernaum, the collectors of the temple tax came to Peter and said, "Does your teacher not pay the temple tax?" He said, "Yes, he does." And when he came home, Jesus spoke of it first, asking, "What do you think, Simon? From whom do kings of the earth take toll or tribute? From their children, or from others?" When Peter said, "From others," Jesus said to him, "Then the children are free. However, so that we do not give offence to them, go to the sea and cast a hook; take the first fish that comes up; and when you open its mouth, you will find a coin; take that and give it to them for you and me."'[94]

What makes the story so incredible is that it seems to show Jesus acting as a wonder-worker operating for his own advantage, something that does not fit into the picture of him that the gospels normally give us. To understand this event, one has to take into account the context in which Matthew writes. Matthew wrote his gospel somewhere between AD 80-90 after the destruction of the Jerusalem temple in AD 70. Before that date some sort of pre-gospel tradition about paying the temple tax may have existed in Matthew's church, a church heavily Jewish in its origins and with Jewish members in Matthew's day. The main point of the story is that Jesus and his disciples are exempt from paying the temple tax because they belong to God's kingdom whereas those not 'in the kingdom' are still bound by the duty of paying the tax. Nonetheless, Jesus and his disciples agree to pay the tax in order not to scandalise their fellow Jews.

There is good reason to believe that the original story ended with the words 'Then the children are free'. Matthew then adds a humorous and folkloric touch by having Jesus provide the money not from the common purse or some rich supporter but from the mouth of a fiscally philanthropic fish! Strictly speaking, no miracle is involved here at all since Matthew does not go on to tell us whether Peter ever did as Jesus seemed to suggest. Matthew loses all interest in the story when he has made his point about the freedom of Jesus and his disciples from paying the tax while stressing the need to balance that freedom with the avoidance of scandal.

However, the fact remains that Jesus is portrayed in the gospels as one who performed extraordinary deeds, a fact also mentioned by the Jewish historian Josephus. Indeed one could go so far as to say that if we do not accept the tradition that Jesus performed such deeds, every other gospel statement about him would have to be regarded as equally unhistorical. Some, of course, would claim that all references to miracles in scripture are simply to be taken metaphorically although there is no sound evidence for such an assumption. Others would claim that the miracles attributed to Jesus are creations of the early church. But given the fact that there is a convergence of so many different miracle stories from so many different sources, there are sound reasons to believe that the historical Jesus performed actions considered by his followers to be miracles.[95] There seems to be no reason why the risen Christ should not perform such actions today, actions that we would consider to be miracles.

Let us look briefly at some of the other miracles that are attributed to Jesus in the gospels and seem so unlikely to people today. The notion that people could be possessed by demons was widespread in the ancient world. Even today such a belief can be found in quite a number of countries in Africa, South America not to mention parts of Europe and North America. While, to some, such an idea may seem preposterous, we may approach the idea with somewhat greater sympathy if we remember that Jesus saw exorcism as part of his overall ministry of healing and liberating people from the illnesses and other evils that beset them. In the first century Mediterranean world, mental illness, psychosomatic diseases, and such things as epilepsy were often attributed to demonic possession. Jesus saw himself as battling against such evils and it would have been quite natural for him to understand this aspect of his ministry in terms of exorcism. One has always to remember that Jesus was a man with the mindset of a first century Jew.

In the gospels we find Jesus healing people who were deaf, who had paralysed limbs, who were suffering from blindness or various skin ailments such as leprosy. To quote but one example: 'When Jesus returned to Capernaum after some days, it was reported that he was at home. So many gathered around that there was no longer room for them, not even in front of the door; and he was speaking the word to them. Then some people came, bringing to him a paralysed man, carried by four of them. And when they could not bring him to Jesus because of the crowd, they removed the roof above him; and after having dug through it, they let down the mat on which the paralytic lay. When Jesus saw their faith, he said to the paralytic, "Son, your sins are forgiven." Now some of the scribes were sitting there, questioning in their hearts. "Why does this fellow speak in this way? It is blasphemy! Who can forgive sins but God alone?" At once Jesus perceived in his spirit that they were discussing these questions among themselves, and he said to them, "Why do you raise such questions in your hearts? Which is easier, to say to the paralytic, 'Your sins are forgiven' or to say 'Stand up and take your mat and walk'? But so that you may know that the Son of Man has authority on earth to forgive sins" – he said to the paralytic - "I say to you, stand up, take your mat and go to your home." And he stood up, and immediately took the mat and went out before all of them, so that they were all amazed and glorified God, saying, "We have never seen anything like this!"'[96]

What are we to make of these and other such miracles related in the gospels? Believers, of course, are open to the idea that Jesus did actually perform miracles or, to be more precise, that God performed miracles through him. Non-believers might think in terms of psychosomatic illnesses that could be cured by hypnosis, autosuggestion or through the impact of a strong charismatic personality. Such suggestions, however, can hardly explain the raising of people from the dead.

Jesus is quoted as saying to John the Baptist's disciples, 'Go and tell John what you hear and see: the blind receive their sight, the lame walk, the lepers are cleansed, the deaf hear, the dead are raised, and the poor have good news brought to them. And blessed is anyone who takes no of-

fense at me.'[97] Jesus makes the claim that, through his instrumentality, even dead people are raised to life. Let us
look at one example.

Jesus 'went to a town called Nain, and his disciples and
a large crowd went with him. As he approached the gate
of the town, a man who had died was being carried out.
He was his mother's only son, and she was a widow; and
with her was a large crowd from the town. When the Lord
saw her, he had compassion for her and he said to her, "Do
not weep." Then he came forward and touched the bier,
and the bearers stood still. And he said, "Young man, I say
to you, rise!" The dead man sat up and began to speak,
and Jesus gave him to his mother. Fear seized all of them;
and they glorified God, saying, "A great prophet has risen
among us!" and "God has looked favourably on his people!" This word about him spread throughout Judea and
all the surrounding country.'[98]

So God, in and through Jesus, does seem to interfere
with the laws of nature from time to time – raising someone
from the dead is one such example. God does so, however,
in very restrained and limited ways. Disasters, both personal and social, keep happening and God does not usually
intervene to put a stop to them. John Polkinghorne makes
the point that 'Christian theology understands God's act
of creation as being a free act of love. Such an act may well
involve the acceptance by its author of some measure of
limitation, a kenosis (emptying) as the theologians say, of
divine power. After all, God's omnipotence can only mean
that he is able to do what he wills *consistent with his nature.*
Love characteristically tempers power of command. Both
the lawful necessity of the world and the role that contin-
gent chance has to play within it are aspects of that great
creative act. Thus in accepting them God may have, in his
freedom, accepted a self-limitation which circumscribes
his mode of action.'[99]

If miracles, such as the raising of dead people, do occur

they must be part of God's action and purpose that goes beyond everyday experience but yet form part of a coherent whole. *The* great miracle of Christianity, the resurrection of Christ from the dead, is something that is certainly beyond our everyday experience, where the dead tend to remain dead! Christ's resurrection, however, is more than simply the raising of a man to life: it is also a sign, an anticipation of what Jesus claims will be the experience of all men and women, of those who 'look for the resurrection of the dead'. The raising of the widow's son in Nain or the raising of Lazarus[100] are other such signs providing an insight into a deeper reality that is not usually perceptible to us, the ultimate destiny of all humanity.

John P. Meier states that a miracle 'is (1) an unusual, startling, or extraordinary event that is in principle perceivable by any interested and fair-minded observer, (2) an event that finds no reasonable explanation in human abilities or in other known forces that operate in our world of time and space, and (3) an event that is the result of a special act of God, doing what no human power can do.'[101] In the Bible, nature was not viewed, as it is today, as a closed system of laws. Storms, famine and plagues were regarded as divine visitations or divine punishments, something not unknown even in some quarters today. There was no awareness of what we call the laws of nature. The Bible pictures events as miraculous that are explicable on the level of human interaction as well as those that are not. For example, the great 'miracle' of the Jewish Testament, the Exodus, spoke of the escape of the Israelites from Egypt thorough the Reed Sea which was a marsh to the north of the Red Sea. This crossing and subsequent drowning of the Egyptian army could be explained by the natural phenomena of tides and winds. Nonetheless the biblical authors saw this event through the eyes of faith and saw in it a miraculous action by God on Israel's behalf. It was not a conjuring trick by God but an act of God's power as he inspired the Israelites to find liberation and salvation from their Egyptian oppressors.

It is Christianity's claim that God was in Christ in a unique way. Given that that is true, it is only to be expected that unprecedented events might happen in his lifetime, because Jesus represented a new order of things in the world.

Time and time again in the gospels miracles are said to occur because of peoples' faith. 'Everything is possible to one who has faith,' Jesus said.[102] Faith is the conviction that God can and will do great things for his people if their faith in God is strong enough. 'Truly I tell you, if you say to this mountain, "Be taken up and thrown into the sea," and if you do not doubt in your heart, but believe that what you say will come to pass, it will be done for you.'[103] Faith is the strong conviction that something can and will happen because God wants it to happen: it is the conviction that God wants what is good for his people and that good will finally triumph over evil, no matter how unlikely that may seem in the present. As the letter to the Hebrews put it: 'Faith is the assurance of things hoped for, the conviction of things not seen.' (11:1)

Jesus regularly commended people's faith and even went so far as to state that it was their faith that healed them.[104] 'On the way to Jerusalem, Jesus was going through the region between Samaria and Galilee. As he entered a village, ten lepers approached him. Keeping their distance, they called out, saying, "Jesus, Master, have mercy on us!" When he saw them, he said to them, "Go and show yourselves to the priests." And as they went they were made clean. Then one of them, when he saw that he was healed, turned back, praising God with a loud voice. He prostrated himself at Jesus' feet and thanked him. And he was a Samaritan. Then Jesus asked, "Were not ten made clean? But the other nine, where are they? Was none of them found to return and give praise to God except this foreigner?" Then he said to him, "Get up and go on your way; *your faith has made you well.*"'[105]

Jesus did not cure all those who were sick, take way all human suffering or raise all those who had died. One reason for this was peoples' lack of faith. 'Jesus came to his hometown and began to teach the people in their synagogue, so that they were astounded and said, "Where did this man get his wisdom and these deeds of power? Is not this the carpenter's son? Is not his mother called Mary? And are not his brothers James and Joseph and Simon and Judas? And are not all his sisters with us? Where did this man get all this?" And they took offence at him. But Jesus said to them, "Prophets are not without honour except in their own country and in their own house." And he did not do many deeds of powers there, *because of their unbelief.*'[106]

Jesus' ability to perform miracles was limited by peoples' lack of faith. Where faith existed, 'windows' for God to be 'powerful' in the human world became possible. When people asked God to intervene in life, this changed the possibilities for God because God always wishes to build a relationship with people. There is a connection here with our own human experience. While God provides us all with our gifts and human possibilities, we are empowered by others' confidence in them and encouragement of them. Something of the divine-human cooperation is evident in all of this.

Jesus' primary *motive* for performing miracles through the power of God was compassion and love for his suffering people. God's one and only desire was to liberate people from their fatalistic resignation to suffering and for the coming of God's reign of justice, peace and love among men and women. However, this would only happen when people had deep faith and when their actions flowed from that faith. Jesus' own faith gave rise to the miraculous success of his efforts. Nor did he think that he had any monopoly over compassion, faith and miraculous cures. On one occasion, 'John said to him, "Teacher, we saw someone casting out demons in your name, and we tried to stop him because he was not following us." But Jesus said, "Do not stop him; for no one who does a deed of power in my name will soon afterward to speak evil of me. Whoever is not against us is with us."'[107] What Jesus wanted to do most of all was to awaken the same compassion and faith in the people around him because that alone would enable the power of God to become operative and effective in their midst.

Jesus' miracles, performed out of compassion and love, always pointed to a fundamental, underlying reality: the coming of God's kingdom so that, over time, it would gradually become a reality in the world through the power of God at work in human hearts. The book of Revelation, in its own poetic fashion, tries to capture the final outcome of the in-breaking of God's kingdom, of which all that Jesus said and did, including his miracles, were but a fore-taste. 'Then I (John) saw a new heaven and a new earth; for the first heaven and the first earth had passed away, and the sea was no more. And I saw the holy city, the new Jerusalem, coming down out of heaven from God, pre-pared as a bride adorned for her husband. And I heard a loud voice from the throne saying, "See, the home of God is among mortals. He will dwell with them as their God; they will be his peoples, and God himself will be with them; he will wipe away every tear from their eyes. Death will be no more; mourning and crying and pain will be no more, for the first things have passed away."'[108]

When we pray, even for miracles, we are praying that God's life and love may reign in peoples' hearts. Sometimes that love is demonstrated in miracles. Let Kitty Ferguson have the last word. 'Science leads us to hope that complete understanding is potentially within the grasp of human collective reason, but science is not overly confident of finding it. John Barrow writes: "There is no formula that can deliver all truth, all harmony, all simplicity. No Theory of Everything can provide total insight. For to see through everything would leave us seeing nothing at all." As St Paul wrote: "Now we see but a poor reflection as in a mirror; then we shall see face to face. Now I know in part; then I shall know fully, even as I am fully known." Religion is far more optimistic than science that in some manner, beyond our present concept of human reason, we can know "everything important." Perhaps the most significant difference between science and religion is that science thinks that on this quest we are entirely on our own. Religion tells us that although we who seek the truth may ride imaginary horses, Truth also seeks *us*.'[109]

Having looked at Jesus' life, teaching, his role as saviour and his miracles, we now turn to the church which has the task of carrying on Christ's mission in the world.

PART 3

Has the Church a Future?

As regards religion there is a completely new atmosphere that conditions its practice. On the one hand people are taking a hard look at all magical worldviews and prevailing superstitions and demanding a more personal and active commitment of faith, so that not a few have achieved a lively sense of the divine. On the other hand greater numbers are falling away from the practice of religion. In the past it was the exception to repudiate God and religion to the point of abandoning them, and then only in individual cases: but nowadays it seems a matter of course to reject them as incompatible with scientific progress and a new kind of humanism. In many places it is not only in philosophical terms that such trends are expressed, but there are signs of them in literature, art, the humanities, the interpretation of history and even civil law: all of which is very disturbing to many people.[1]

CHAPTER 12

A Sense of Belonging

'If basic communities gradually become indispensable – otherwise, in the present situation and that of the immediate future, the institutional church will shrivel up into a church without people – the Episcopal great church has the task and duty of stimulating and of contributing to their formation and their necessary missionary activity. If the basic community is really Christian and genuinely alive, the result of a free decision of faith in the midst of a secularised world where Christianity can scarcely be handed on any longer by the power of social tradition, then all ecclesiastical organisation is largely at the service of these communities: they are not means to serve the ends of an ecclesiastical bureaucracy defending and wanting to reproduce itself.'[2]

As we noted in our introduction, the church has been affected by the 'faith' that people place in science and the capitalist ethic as well as by the disintegration of traditional communities and value systems. Bishops and priests speak of the church as the Christian community but one has to ask whether the church, as we experience it today is, in any real sense, a genuine community?

The 'hungers of the heart' cry out today for a new connectedness, a new sense of belonging, of communion, of community, but people all too easily apply the word 'community' to almost any collection of individuals – a town, a church, an apartment complex, a professional body, regardless of how well or how poorly people relate to or communicate with each other. 'If we are going to use the

word meaningfully, we must restrict it to a group of individuals who have learned to go deeper than their masks of
composure, and have developed some significant commitment to rejoice together, mourn together, delight in each
other and make others' conditions our own.'³

Community exists when people are committed to one
another and share common goals. They have a sense of
purpose that gives coherence and meaning to what they
do *together*. Such a sense of purpose may simply be the
scratching out of subsistence for themselves and their families in the realisation that only through common effort will
they be able to survive.

In community, people are prepared to communicate
honestly with one another. Such communication and sharing never comes easily; it can be a difficult and even
painful process but without it a community is such only in
name. To achieve real communication means giving time
and effort to listening to and sharing with others non-
judgementally. While there will always be differences of
personality, gender, education, and socio-economic back-
ground, people strive to transcend such individual differences by making time and giving commitment to genuine
listening and sharing. It is not simply a question of voting
or of one person taking all the decisions but rather a seeking of consensus so that everyone is involved in the decision-making process.

In community, people should be free to speak their
minds, to share their hopes and fears, their faith and
doubts. They should even be allowed to go against the
trend. The resulting consensus, born of many differing
viewpoints, is more effective in motivating people than
decision-making by one or two people because a wider
view of the challenges to be faced is gained than can be
achieved by the few.

When people are truly 'in communion', they tend to
grow in realism and humility. Experiencing the talents and

limitations, the joys and sorrows of other peoples' lives, they see their own lives in a truer perspective. Individualism is often arrogant but when other peoples' gifts or brokenness are appreciated, people become aware of their own gifts and brokenness also and arrogance is diminished.

In community, old wounds can be healed, old resentments forgotten, old resistances overcome, though not without effort. The extraordinary thing is that where genuine community is fostered, when people communicate in some depth, healing and conversion can and do happen. It is not that people are trying to convert or heal one another but rather, in accepting others as they are and not trying to change them, people are able to heal themselves. Acceptance by others is like good soil that permits wheat to grow and develop to the full. Acceptance enables people to become their true selves because it releases in them a capacity to grow. If a community provides the soil of acceptance, it enables people to realise their humanity more fully, to accept both their talents and their limitations, their joys as well as their sorrows. They are free to be themselves and then they can discard their defences, their masks and their disguises. They become free to seek their own psychological and spiritual health because, above all, the community provides them with the inner feeling of being loved. To be accepted as one is, is a real act of love because to feel accepted is to feel loved. To feel loved is to feel part of a community, connected to others in ways that give life.[4]

The basic unit of the church 'community' has been the parish. Large parishes, often handling hundreds of people on a Sunday, do not generally possess any real sense of community. They need to be broken down, at least functionally, into smaller, basic groups where people can relate to one another and to the Lord in ways that are life giving.[5] We often pray to God 'who unites us in love', but the fact is that, for much of the time, we are nowhere close to such unity- in-love at all.

Unless Christians share together a vision that energises them and gives them a sense of meaning and purpose, they can very easily succumb to the idea that production, consumption and final extinction are all that there is to life. 'Eat, drink and be merry for tomorrow we die.'

In the past, as Karen Armstrong has pointed out, people were sustained by two ways of thinking, speaking and acquiring knowledge, which scholars called *mythos* and *logos*. Myth was not concerned with practical matters, but with meaning. 'The *mythos* of a society provided people with a context that made sense of their day-to-day lives; it directed their attention to the eternal and the universal. It was also rooted in what we call the unconscious mind. The various mythological stories, *which were not intended to be taken literally*, were an ancient form of psychology.'[6]

One such 'myth', for example, was the creation story in the Book of Genesis. It was not as if the ancients literally believed that God created the world in seven days. Rather they saw the creation story as a means of 'capturing' the truth that God was the creator of all things including the human family and encapsulating this in story form.

Logos, on the other hand, was the rational, pragmatic, and scientific thought that enabled men and women to function well in the world. Modern men and women tend to give pride of place to *Logos*. For the ancients, both *mythos* and *logos* were essential elements that gave meaning to as well as practical direction to life.

Christ's great vision, which should give meaning and purpose to any Christian community and to the church as a whole, is the coming of God's kingdom where men and women live as brothers and sisters, united by the Spirit with Jesus Christ as sons and daughters of the Father and in harmony with the whole of the created universe. Part of that 'coming' is the creation of communities of faith, hope and love that bear witness to the gradual realisation of God's dream for humanity.

But, almost as soon as our hearts are stirred by God's vision, another voice is heard telling us that it is all a pipe dream. 'In our dog-eat-dog world, if you place your trust in others you are a loser. Competition is the name of the game. The Self-made, Self-reliant Man is god.' Personal, racial, ethnic, national and religious prejudices are endemic to our world. Strangers are to be feared because they may be potential enemies, before even a word is exchanged. So we become defensive, unable to be our true selves and unable to reach out to others. Hence the coming of God's kingdom seems well nigh impossible.

One is reminded of the cry of the apostles, 'Who then can be saved?' The only response we will get is the one given by Jesus: 'For mortals it is impossible, but not for God; for God all things are possible.'[7] Jesus does not water down the challenge or alter reality because it is too difficult. It *is* difficult to enter into God's dream for the world but not impossible. Everything is possible, Jesus says, to the one who has faith, to the one who puts his or her trust in God's love and seeks to love one's neighbour as oneself.

One reason why community building is so difficult for Christians is fear – fear not only of the vulnerability involved in reaching out to others, but fear of following in the footsteps of the truly human, as well as divine, Jesus. Christians have tended to concentrate so much on the divinity of Jesus, seeing him as 'up there in the clouds' and leaving us down here to scratch out an existence according to the rules of the market place, that they fail to see the implications of following him in his humanity. In three of the gospels, Jesus is quoted as saying, 'If anyone wishes to come after me, he must deny himself and take up his cross daily and follow me.'[8] In other words, if Jesus has to suffer, so also will his followers. Forming and sustaining communities of faith, hope and love that reach out to everyone, but especially to the poor and the powerless, will inevitably invite opposition from those who prefer to maintain the status quo or put the pursuit of money, power, prestige, self and career above the well-being of God's 'little ones'. Disturbing the comfortable is always a dangerous occupation.

As basic Christian communities 'tune into' and act out of God's dream, providing themselves with a sense of meaning and purpose that mere 'getting and spending' can never provide, they can find ways of counteracting society's dehumanising tendencies by enabling people to challenge the values of the consumer society through fidelity to a life of shared faith, shared prayer, shared sacramental practice, mutual encouragement and mutual support.

However, the breakdown of community in secular society has added to a trend within the church itself that has been happening over centuries, namely the 'privatisation' of faith and of sacramental practice. People who regard themselves as fully committed Christians often do so simply because they go to church on Sunday, take part in one or other of the sacraments from time to time, and give to this or that charity. Faith is seen as a purely personal matter, a private affair between oneself and God. God, such people believe, is primarily concerned with one's goodness or guilt and reward or punishment in the next life. They fail to see that to be a disciple of Christ involves communal involvement with others. 'For just as the body is one and has many members, and all the members of the body, though many, are one body, so it is with Christ. For in the one Spirit we were all baptised into one body – Jews or Greeks, slaves or free – and we were all made to drink of one Spirit. Indeed, the body does not consist of one member, but of many.'[9]

Faith, seen as a purely private affair between oneself and God and leading to reward in the next life, reeks of 'pie-in-the-sky-when-you-die'. It is hardly good news for those who are shunted to the margins of the world of the

well-off and made to suffer, in euphemistic military language, 'consequential collateral damage'! It is significant,
and should be a warning to the church, that God's beloved
poor, in the western world at least, have largely given up
on the church.

The Acts of the Apostles tells us that the first Christians
'devoted themselves to the teaching of the apostles and to
the communal life, to the breaking of bread and to the
prayers.'[10] They belonged to what they called the *koinonia*,
by which they meant that they possessed strong bonds of
fellowship and of communion both with the risen Christ
and with one another. While we should not exaggerate
this sense of community, which would fracture time and
again in the history of the church, even in its earliest days,
nonetheless such *koinonia* bears witness to true discipleship. 'By this everyone will know that you are my disciples, if you have love for one another.'[11] What was true at
the beginning of Christianity remains true today. Unless
Christians are seen to love one another, rejoice together,
mourn together, delight in each other, as well as pray together, 'break bread' together, 'give thanks' together and
'bring good news to the poor' together, they will hardly be
given much credence in the twenty-first century.

Christian mystics speak of their wordless and image-
less experiences of God that surpass all human concepts.
This mystic tradition of the church should alert us to the
fact that when we use the word 'God' we never capture the
full reality of God anymore than when we speak of the Son
of God we capture the full reality of Jesus. God is beyond
our knowing except insofar as he chooses to reveal himself
to us. This God does through the experiences of the Jewish
people as recorded in the Jewish scriptures and through
the experiences of the first disciples' encounter with Jesus
as revealed in the Christian scriptures, as well as through
our own faith experiences.

The Jewish scriptures, the Law and the Prophets,

formed the hearts and minds of all Jews. Jesus and his first disciples were no exception. However, Jesus sometimes modified Jewish interpretations of the Law. This was remembered by his disciples and became the nucleus of a special teaching. As Christian preachers passed on this special teaching they would add their own teaching by addressing situations that Jesus had never encountered.[12] Such teaching came to be known as the *Teaching of the Apostles* and formed the basis of the Christian scriptures that we know as the New Testament.

Reflection, meditation on and contemplation of the sacred scriptures and what they say to life's experiences are central to the life of any genuine Christian community. People need space in a noise-polluted world to create an inward stillness so that they can take their search for God and God's Word seriously. People need to be able to confront the gospel message, reflect on it and compare it with their own life situations, seeing what import it has for them and for their mission to the world. Pulpit preaching alone can never replace such 'confrontation'.

We see one small example of such 'confrontation' in a passage from St Luke's gospel. Luke recounts the appearance of Jesus to two disciples on the road to Emmaus. (ch. 24) This embryonic little community was crushed by Jesus' crucifixion and, as they made their way to Emmaus, they discussed all that had happened in Jerusalem. 'We were hoping that he (Jesus) would be the one to redeem Israel.' Suddenly a stranger appears in their midst and gradually their understanding is changed. Jesus, for he is indeed the stranger, 'beginning with Moses and all the prophets, interpreted to them what referred to him in the scriptures.' 'Was it not necessary that the Messiah should suffer all these things and enter into his glory?' Jesus went back over the texts of scripture in order to help the disciples understand their present situation. Now they began to see the crucifixion in a new light. When Jesus entered the house where they were staying, he took bread, said the blessing and broke it and suddenly they recognised him in the breaking of bread. Afterwards they said to each other, *'were not our hearts burning while he spoke to us on the way and opened the scriptures to us?'* The disciples, reflecting on what Jesus had said and comparing it to their previous hopelessness, hurried back to Jerusalem to share their 'good news' with the other disciples. The interpretation of scripture that they had heard enabled them to see the meaning of their *present situation* and gain hope for the future.

By reflecting on and praying the scriptures and seeing how their own lives conform to God's Word, Christians not only discover how best to be at one with God and live together in mutual love but also how best to address the grief and anguish of God's beloved poor. When any Christian community, or the wider church for that matter, fails to take account of human suffering, it soon becomes self-preoccupied and selfish.

Praying for each other was another aspect of *koinonia*. St Paul's letters contain many references to his constant prayers for the communities he founded. But prayer means more than just 'saying prayers'. Prayer, as both a personal and communal conscious relationship with God, enables a community to realise that God's Spirit is at work in its midst helping it to draw out the implications of what Jesus said and did and pointing to ways of how best to serve others, even those with little or no religious affiliation, in simplicity, in honesty, in truth and most of all in love.

While there is a new and widespread openness to spiritual searching today, this tends to take place *outside the mainstream churches.* The riches of spiritual contemplation and meditation that grew up in the church over the centuries, enabling people to experience God in their lives, were, by and large, the preserve of religious and the clergy. Most members of the church were seldom taught that they too could, both personally and collectively, hear God 'speak' in their hearts. As a consequence, many people have now turned to eastern religions or New Age philosophies to find their spiritual sustenance. While spirituality is very much in vogue, with its myriad of therapies, meditation techniques, regimes of holistic living and so on, all this is usually detached from an explicitly religious expression.

Each Christian community also needs to discern the injustices that may lie at the heart of the community itself. We see an example of this in chapter six of the Acts of the Apostles. 'At that time, as the number of disciples continued to grow, the Hellenists (Palestinian Jews who spoke Greek) complained against the Hebrews because their widows were being neglected in the daily distribution. So the Twelve called together the community of the disciples and said, "It is not right for us to neglect the word of God to serve at table. Brothers, select from among you seven reputable men, filled with the Spirit and wisdom, whom we shall appoint to this task, whereas we shall devote ourselves to prayer and to the ministry of the word." The proposal was acceptable to the whole community, so they chose Stephen, a man filled with faith and the Holy Spirit, also Philip, Prochorus, Nicanor, Timon, Parmenas, and Nicholas of Antioch, a convert to Judaism. They presented these men to the apostles who prayed and laid hands on them.'[13]

Present day communities, priests and people together, need to discern, for example, the rightful place of women and those who live on the margins of our society, God's beloved poor, in the decision-making processes of the church. Questions concerning the crisis of identity among priests, the future of priestly celibacy, the authority crisis in the church, the lack of theological and spiritual formation among ordinary Christians, the involvement of priests in sexual abuse, and so on and so forth, all cry out

for answers in the present day church. In basic or cell communities everyone should be involved in the decision-
making processes and in seeking answers to the problems
that face the church today because such involvement gives
church leaders a greater sense of what the faithful are
thinking and experiencing and gives people a proper
sense of dignity and the feeling that all have a part to play
in the on-going mission of Christ.

Effective Christian communities of the future will be
more than mere groups of sympathisers, still less mere
congregations of people with little in common. They will
be local groups of people who, knowing each other in
some depth, seek to build a common fellowship with one
another and with Christ in realising God's dream for the
world. They will no longer be mere 'gospel consumers',
passive receptors of the preached word, but 'gospel cre-
ators', men and women who not only hear and seek to understand the word of God but, 'reading the signs of the
times', seek to put it into practice.

Christian communities have a duty to maintain unity
with the whole church, not developing sectarian or heretical theologies of their own. They must be guided by the
bishops of the church who have the important duty of har-
monising evangelical interpretations into a unity that respects diversity within the framework of one faith, one
baptism, and one church. They must be open, in a self-critical spirit, to other communities beyond their own fron-
tiers and make vital contacts with them because some of
the essential tasks of the greater church will go beyond the
resources of any one community.

However, if the institutional church is not to shrivel up
into a church without people, especially the poor, the
formation of basic communities is indispensable, otherwise Christians will go on living in isolation from each
other, trying to make their lonely way to God. One of the
most important tasks, therefore, of the Episcopate is to

encourage the growth of such communities. More than ever, Christians need such communities if they are to make free decisions of faith in the midst of an unbelieving world. Those who follow Christ need a sense of belonging, of communion, of discipleship with the risen Christ and with one another if they are to assist the whole church in carrying on Christ's mission. They need to find ways of rejoicing together, mourning together, delighting in each other, praying together, 'breaking bread', giving thanks and serving their neighbours together. They need to form themselves into '*a community of people* united in Christ and guided by the Holy Spirit in their pilgrimage toward the Father's kingdom, bearers of a message for all humanity. That is why they cherish a feeling of solidarity with the human race and its history.'[14]

Cardinal Kim of Korea said in a homily that 'the essence of the good news is – giving. The "official church" does not reflect this "total giving", this continuous "self-emptying" of Jesus. Rather, very often, she gives the impression of the opposite: of being entrenched, of guarding and protecting what she has. She does not project a consistent and effective impression of giving her life for the world. The "this-worldly" elements in the church fall into the fallacy of almost every large corporation: spending too much energy on keeping the institution alive, or on expanding it. The church falls into the error of trying to increase herself rather than to increase the flock. Jesus gave himself as food for the life of the world. Insofar as maintaining and expanding the status quo of the *institution* is her major concern, the church is reversing the process and feeds upon the flock to increase her own institutional life.'

M. Scott Peck, writing about the creation of community in his book *The Different Drum*, quotes from Keith Miller's *The Scent of Love*. Miller proposes a reason why the early Christians were such phenomenally successful evangelists: 'It was not because of their charisms – such as the gift

of speaking in tongues – and not because Christianity was
such a palatable doctrine (to the contrary, it is about the
most unpalatable doctrine there is) but because they had
discovered the secret of community. Generally they did
not have to lift a finger to evangelise. Someone would be
walking down a back alley in Corinth or Ephesus and
would see a group of people sitting together talking about
the strangest things – something about a man and a tree
and an execution and an empty tomb. What they were
talking about made no sense to the onlooker. But there was
something about the way they spoke to each other, about
the way they cried together, the way they laughed together,
the way they touched one another that was strangely appealing. It gave off what Miller called the scent of love. The
onlooker would start to drift farther down the alley, only
to be pulled back to this little group like a bee to a flower.
He would listen some more, still not understanding, and
start to drift away again. But again he would be pulled
back, thinking I don't have the slightest idea of what these
people are talking about, but whatever it is, I want part of
it.'

Scott Peck adds: 'This might have seemed to me merely
one author's romantic imaginings had I not myself witnessed the phenomenon in action. I have led community-
building groups in the most sterile hotels, yet desk clerks
and barmaids will stop me or other members and say, "I
don't know what you people are doing in there, but I get
off duty at three o'clock. Can I join you?"'[15]

At the heart of any genuine Christian community,
sacramental life should play an essential role. But many
young people, and indeed many who are not so young,
have simply given up on the church and its sacramental
life. Why is this so?

CHAPTER 13

Strangers after Communion

The renewal of the church, begun at Vatican II, initiated liturgical reform and for the first time the man and woman in the pew could hear the sacramental words in his or her own language. Such a development has had some unforeseen consequences. What was seen as mysterious before, providing people with some sense of the mystery of God became, for some, merely banal ritual. For others, the sacramental life of the church began to seem more akin to magic. A magical worldview exists where no natural relationship can be seen between something we do and the outcome that results. So, for example, hopping around on one foot in the expectation that such activity will make the gods produce rain is magical. Magic is using words and / or gestures that *compel* superhuman powers to solve human problems.

The early Christians did not practise magic or offer sacrifices. In order not to be labelled atheists among their Jewish brethren, they spoke of Jesus' words and actions at the Last Supper in terms of 'offering' and 'sacrifice'. However, what Jesus was offering was not sacrifice in the traditional sense but his own life on behalf of others. He was put to death because he claimed to speak in God's name and spoke out against the many injustices meted out to the poor and the downtrodden.

So if sacraments are not mere rituals or magic, what is their role in the life of the church? In order to place them in context, we must begin with the resurrection of Christ that proved to be such a major 'transforming experience' for the disciples. 'From time to time people do have experiences which deeply affect and influence their lives. One thinks for example of those rich experiences associated with special moments of fellowship, reconciliation, and solidarity. These kinds of experiences, in virtue of their gratuity, do in fact disarm and surprise, lift and renew, change and transform our lives. In a similar way the transcendent power of the risen Jesus was experienced by the apostles as a gracious fellowship, a personal reconciliation and a divine solidarity which did in fact disarm and surprise, lift and renew, change and transforms their lives. It is no mere coincidence that many of the resurrection narratives are written up in a language that is in fact trying to describe these kinds of rich experiences.'[16]

After the resurrection the disciples experienced the power of Christ's presence among them and were convinced that he was still guiding and inspiring them through the power of the Spirit he had promised them. 'I will ask the Father, and he will give you another advocate to be with you always. The advocate will teach you everything and remind you of all that I told you.'[17] God's Spirit cannot be separated from God; it is not some magical substance separate from God but is God near to, within, inspiring, guiding the Christian community by teaching men and women of all generations the implications of who Jesus is and what he did and said.

Some of the work of God's Spirit is made visible within the Christian community through the signs and gestures we call sacraments. The early church saw nothing but faith in these communitarian gestures: faith in the plain state and faith expressed in signs and symbolic gestures were one and the same reality. A kiss or the giving of flowers can be tangible signs and symbols of love but they are not love itself: they are simply symbols of love offered. Such gestures demand trust and faith on the part of the recipients that the person making the gesture truly loves them.

In somewhat similar fashion, sacramental signs and symbols point to and make tangible God's gracious act of self-giving in love in the person of the risen Christ who continues to dwell in the midst of his faith-filled community. In the sacramental signs and symbols the reality of Christ's presence is made manifest, even more so than in our human gestures of sending flowers or expressing human affection. In the Eucharist the sign becomes the reality of the presence of the risen Christ. Hence the sacraments are interpersonal encounters between the *believing community* and the risen Lord. 'Where two or three are gathered in my name, there am I in the midst of them.'[18] But, having privatised faith, this communal sense of what sacraments are about is often lost.

Sacramental signs call for a response to God's love and the forging of loving and compassionate relationships within the community itself. More than that, by participating in the sacramental activity of the church, the community should be strengthened to carry on Christ's work of reconciliation and liberation more effectively. Sacramental activity is 'counter-cultural' in the sense that, by participating in the sacramental life of the church, one asserts that life is about more than getting and spending: it is about commitment and loving service.

The sacraments are signs and gestures 'instituted' by Christ in the sense that initiation into the community, the forgiveness of sin, the gift of the Spirit, the enduring presence of Christ in his self-offering to the Father, the healing of the sick, the call for radical commitment in marriage, the call to act as ministers of the word and as leaders of the community, are all to be found in Jesus' own ministry.

Just as there are significant moments or turning points in the life of every individual – birth, growing up, coping with human relationships, marrying, and growing old and dying – so there are similar moments within the Christian community which become effective signs of the presence and grace of the living Christ.

The church's sacraments are not mere rituals. They should be creative moments of encounter of the whole community in faith with the glorified Christ who communicates with his people by way of efficacious signs and gestures. 'Just as when a drummer is playing he is extending himself through all his bodiliness into the instruments grouped about him, so that these instruments dynamically participate in the expressiveness of his rhythmic movement, making but one total movement which, arising from within the drummer, flows through the rhythm of his body, of his beating hands and stamping feet and produces a varied harmony of percussion – so too the heavenly saving will of Christ, through his glorified body, makes one dynamic unity with the ritual gesture and the sacramental words of the minister who intends to do what the church does. It is only when a person's love is manifested in some telling and appealing gesture, through which it becomes possible for me to enter into this love, that I become personally confronted with this love for me.'[19]

Christ himself is *the* Sacrament, the revelation of God's love and concern for humanity. The church's sacraments are the God-man's expressions of his love and if members of the Christian community are open to accepting that love they encounter the living God, even if it is only 'as in a glass darkly'. One cannot understand sacramental practice unless one sees it as an expression of the faith of the *ecclesial* community, as an expression of God's love revealed and God's life-changing love accepted by his disciples. Let us look very briefly at the church's sacraments.

Baptism is a sign of integration into the community, the earthly embodiment of the dead and risen Lord, drawing people into the life-circle of Christ. St Paul, speaking of baptism, for example, wrote: 'For in one Spirit we were all baptised into one body, whether Jews or Greeks, slaves or free persons, and we were all given the one Spirit.' 'Now you are Christ's body, and individually parts of it.' Paul then goes on to spell out the implications for the followers of Christ who form this one body: 'Some people God has designated in the church to be, first, apostles; second, prophets; third, teachers; then, mighty deeds; then gifts of healing, assistance, administration, and varieties of tongues.' Paul also says that 'if one part (of the body) suffers, all the parts suffer with it; if one part is honoured, all the parts share its joy.'[20]

Confirmation should be a moment of mature commitment, of adult initiation into the mission of the Christian community after a period of years of formation in the practice of the faith. 'You will receive power when the Holy Spirit comes upon you, and *you will be my witnesses in Jerusalem, throughout Judea and Samaria, and to the ends of the earth.*'[21] Young men and women are called upon to dedicate themselves to fashioning their lives in the manner of Jesus' living and dying. They are called to follow the promptings of his Spirit by giving their lives to the world in service rather than in domination, in healing rather than in violence, in love rather than in hate.

In the sacrament of *Reconciliation* people seek healing for the fissures in their own lives and in their relationships with God and with others. Reconciliation also signifies reintegration into the life-giving circle of Christ, the Christian community, of those who have become estranged. When people acknowledge their need to forgive and be forgiven, they acknowledge their own sinfulness and seek once more to live out their relationships in absolute honesty. In confessing to a priest, who represents Christ united with his community of faith, one acknowledges that sin has both social as well as personal consequences. Reconciliation is never simply a private matter between oneself and God: it is always a *communal* reality.

'It has to be admitted by church people that the failures of past confessional practice, the compulsions and obsessiveness associated with the Sacrament of Penance ("religious scruples"), the frequently induced fear and lack of compassion, the distorted focusing of all morality upon sex, and the scandalous inadequacies of priests, have often diminished the healing power of this sacrament. But the tragedy is that in a time when the actions of self-revelation, acceptance, honesty, and forgiveness are so desperately needed, it is precisely this sacrament which is least practised. Its full reconciling force will never be experienced unless we ask for and grant forgiveness for past mistakes and sins and proceed to see its social, political, and cultural significance for the present. To confess one's sins is not only the beginning of a change of heart: it is a liberation from servitude to cultural pretence.'[22]

In a culture that tries to cover over the reality of death and dying, *anointing the sick* signifies that death is real but not the last word. We know in faith that we are loved beings and that we can enter into the dying of Christ with trusting abandonment. The strength that Christ gives to those who are seriously ill, through God's Spirit at work in the community that stands with the sick and dying, can enable people to face even death fearlessly.

The sacrament of *Orders* provides servant-leaders who 'tend the Word of God', and build community solidarity. We will return to the question of priesthood in our final chapter.

Christian *marriage* signifies the sharing by two people of their love, their desire for the deepest union possible, and a sharing of that love by co-creating new life, in a mutual life-long commitment, imaging Christ's relationship to his people. Such life-long human commitment is profoundly counter-cultural in today's world.

The first Christians were Jews who continued to attend worship in the temple. 'Every day they devoted themselves to meeting together in the temple area and to breaking bread in their homes.'[23] This sacred meal, eaten only by those who believed in Jesus, was a major way of showing *koinonia*, fellowship, communion with the risen Lord and with one another and eventually was what helped to make Christians feel distinct from other Jews. Just as the *Eucharist* was central to the life of the early Christians, so it must be for any modern community.

The Eucharist signifies loving union with the risen Christ who gives himself to his disciples in a real, living, personal presence experienced in faith. In being present to them, Christ unites them with his own self-giving to the Father on behalf of sinners and, at the same time, deepens their loving union with each other so that they can share more effectively in Christ's mission. The sacramental bread and wine not only makes Christ's presence real but is also the sign that brings about the real presence of the church to Christ and makes the church the body of Christ.

Nowhere is the tendency to regard the sacraments in al-most magical terms clearer than in present-day celebra-tions of the Lord's Supper. People 'go up to communion', we say, failing to notice the contradiction in terms. Each person goes 'up to communion' surrounded by people who are more or less strangers and who may well continue to be strangers even after 'communion'! The act and fact of receiving communion does not automatically unite people or forge mutual involvement in each other's lives.

The three synoptic gospels speak about the institution of the Eucharist. St Luke, for example, reports that 'Jesus took the bread, said the blessing, broke it, and gave it to his disciples, saying "This is my body, which will be given for you; *do this in memory of me.*"' (22:19) What Jesus was doing was not merely asking his disciples to repeat what he had done at the Last Supper in ritual fashion. Rather it was an invitation to remember what he had done and, as his disci-ples, to imitate him by giving their lives in loving service to the Father and to others, especially those on the margins of society, even to the point of death if that was what was required to further God's reign.

While the other gospels tell us what happened at the Last Supper, St John's gospel speaks instead of its fulfilment and its full realisation. In chapter thirteen John relates the incident where Jesus washes his disciples feet. It is worth quoting John in full:

'It was now the day before the Passover Festival. Jesus knew that the hour had come for him to leave this world and go to the Father. He had always loved those in the world who were his own, and he loved them to the very end. Jesus and his disciples were at supper. The Devil had already put the thought of betraying Jesus into the heart of Judas, the son of Simon Iscariot. Jesus knew that the Father had given him complete power; he knew that he had come from God and was going to God. So he rose from the table, took off his outer garment, and tied a towel around his waist. Then he poured some water into a washbasin and began to wash his disciples feet and dry them with the towel around his waist. He came to Simon Peter, who said to him, "Are you going to wash my feet, Lord?" Jesus answered him, "You do not understand now what I am doing, but you will understand later." Peter declared, "Never at any time will you wash my feet!" "If I do not wash your feet," Jesus answered, "you will no longer be my disciple. Simon Peter answered, "Lord, do not wash only my feet, then! Wash my hands and head too!" Jesus said, "Anyone who has taken a bath is completely clean and does not have to wash himself, except for his feet. All of you are clean – all except one." (Jesus already knew who was going to betray him; that is why he said, "All of you, except one, are clean".)

'After Jesus had washed their feet, he put his outer garment back on and returned to his place at the table. "Do you understand what I have just done to you?" he asked. "You call me Teacher and Lord, and it is right that you do so, because that is what I am. I, your Lord and Teacher, have just washed your feet. You, then, should wash one another's feet. I have set an example for you, so that you will do just what I have done for you. I am telling you the truth: no slave is greater than his master, and no messenger is greater than the one who sent him. Now that you know the truth, how happy you will be if you put it into practice!'"[24]

In Palestine, people went barefoot in sandals, so washing one's feet was important. Rabbis would not allow their disciples to wash their feet: either they did it themselves or had them washed by a servant or a slave. Foot washing was menial slaves' work. Yet here we have Jesus doing the work of a menial slave. For Peter this was too much. He refused to see Jesus in the role of a servant or a slave. In a society where rank and status and the rules of fashion were dominant, we can well understand Peter's refusal. What Jesus did was quite simply too shocking: it overthrew the accepted social order. Again and again in the gospels, we find Jesus using such shock tactics in an effort to get his disciples to see things in a new way and to change their old habits.

Jesus provided a model for his disciples. Among his followers there were to be no master-slave relationships. 'You know that the rulers of the Gentiles lord it over them, and the great ones make their authority felt. But it shall not be so among you. Rather, whoever wishes to be great among you shall be your servant; whoever wishes to be first among you shall be your slave. Just so, the Son of Man did not come to be served but to serve and give his life as a ransom for many.'[25] Jesus made this point clearly when he washed his disciples' feet in the manner of a slave. His disciples were to love and serve each other humbly and then turn that love and service, demonstrated within the community, into an impetus for the loving service of others, especially the poor and downtrodden.

Where there is division in the community, reconciliation has to take place before it can offer its gifts to God.

Jesus said: 'If you bring your gift to the altar, and there re-
call that your brother has anything against you, leave your
gift there at the altar, go first and be reconciled with your
brother, and then come and offer your gift.'[26] This reconciliation is not something that can be accomplished in a few
minutes at the beginning of Mass. 'When we realise that
the grievance of two-thirds of mankind against the other
one-third is the fact of not being able to satisfy their
hunger, we may well ask ourselves: Will a five-minute in-
terruption in our sacramental life be enough to reconcile
us? Will a whole lifetime be enough?'[27]

The earliest accounts of the Lord's Supper occur in the
writings of St Paul. Writing in his first letter to the
Corinthians, he speaks of the divisions among community
members. 'First of all, I hear that when you meet as a
church there are divisions among you, and to a degree I
believe it; there have to be factions among you in order
that those who are approved among you may become
known. When you meet in one place, then, it is not to eat
the Lord's supper, for in eating, each one goes ahead with
his own supper, and one goes hungry while another gets
drunk. Do you not have houses in which you can eat and
drink? Or do you show contempt for the church of God
and make those who have nothing feel ashamed?' (11:18f)
The early Christians met in one another's houses to celebrate the Lord's Supper. The wealthier members of the
community would arrive early and begin to eat a meal before the actual Eucharistic celebration of the 'breaking of
bread' and the 'blessing of the cup'. The poorer members
of the church, who had worked all day without eating,
were excluded and went hungry, suffering the humiliation
of dependency because of the contemptuous neglect of
their richer brothers. The whole purpose of the 'breaking
of bread' was *koinonia*, not division of the community. Paul
insisted that, even though the ritual words were spoken,
the lack of sharing between the rich and poor members of

the community meant that, in reality, there was no Eucharist. What unites the Christian community is possession of the Spirit of Christ and 'whoever does not have the Spirit of Christ does not belong to him.'[28] When Christ's Spirit of unity-in-love is lacking, when the Christian community is fractured, when rich Christians of the northern hemisphere eat their fill while many of their brothers and sisters elsewhere go hungry, can the Lord's Supper take place fruitfully?

The Second Vatican Council, in its *Pastoral Constitution on the Church in the Modern World*, sums up the meaning of the Eucharistic celebration beautifully: 'The Word of God, through whom all things were made, became man and dwelt among us, a perfect man, he entered world history, taking that history into himself and recapitulating it. He reveals to us that God is love (1 John 4:8) and at the same time teaches that the fundamental law of human perfection, and consequently of the transformation of the world, is the new commandment of love. He assures those who trust in the charity of God that the way of love is open to all and that the effort to establish a universal communion will not be in vain.

'This love is not something reserved for important matters, but must be exercised above all in the ordinary circumstances of daily life. Christ's example in dying for us sinners teaches us that we must carry the cross, which the flesh and the world inflict on the shoulders of any who seek after peace and justice. Constituted Lord by his resurrection and given all authority in heaven and on earth, Christ is now at work in human hearts by the power of his Spirit; not only does he arouse in them a desire for the world to come but he quickens, purifies, and strengthens the generous aspirations of humanity to make life more humane and conquer the earth for this purpose. The gifts of the Spirit are manifold: some are called to testify openly to humanity's yearning for its heavenly home and to keep the awareness of it before people's minds; others are called to dedicate themselves to the service of people on earth and in this way to prepare the way for the kingdom of heaven. But the Spirit makes all of them free, ready to put aside love of self and assume earthly resources into human life, stretching out towards that future day when humanity itself will become an offering acceptable to God.

'Christ left his followers a pledge of this hope and food for the journey in the sacrament of faith, in which natural elements, the fruits of human cultivation, are changed into his glorified Body and Blood, as a supper of brotherly and sisterly communion and a foretaste of the heavenly banquet.'[29]

It is clear from the words Jesus used at the Last Supper, 'Take and eat, this is my body', that the crucified, dead and risen Christ becomes present to us in a meal. The primary sacramental form of the Eucharist is therefore not simply 'bread and wine' but a meal in which bread and wine are essential components. This meal is at one and the same time, a remembrance of what Jesus did historically on the cross, not insofar as it is past, but insofar as Christ continues to unite his disciples to his own self-giving in love to the Father until the end of time. Such a meal should be an expression of personal intimacy with Christ that calls for fraternal solidarity and intimacy among his followers. Such solidarity must include those who suffer from a lack of self-esteem, those who are addicted in any way, those who have been abused, bullied or humiliated, indeed all those on the margins of so-called 'polite' society. It is this sort of intimacy with Christ in his self-offering that forms Christ's followers into a real church. Insofar as that solidarity is lacking, a church, a Christian community, is such only in name.[30]

Today sacraments are received *individually* and, even though many people may be present at the celebration, they are not perceived as specifically communal activities.

Given the many obstacles to faith that are thrown up by our ruggedly individualistic, consumerist culture, Christians need to be part of counter-cultural communities that value and foster faith, hope, fidelity, wonder in the face of God's creation, a deep appreciation of God's activity in the hearts and minds of men and women and, above all, a compassionate, mutual love for the poor, the oppressed, the lost and the vulnerable. If people were invited to be part of such communities, sacramental activity might mean more to the men and women of our day.

CHAPTER 14

Lumbering Dinosaurs

Although every priest I know wishes there were more vocations, I know of very few who encourage vocations. I have heard many say that if a young man came to them and said that he wanted to be a priest, they are not sure they would encourage him to do so. That is incredibly telling! Do we simply see ourselves as dinosaurs, lumbering our way into eternal life/extinction? Are we too sterile, old, tired to build a future? Have we decided that if God wants a church, He will have to do the work – forgetting about his hope for our cooperation? (A Parish Priest)

Coming to terms with the full implications of Vatican II over the past thirty years has been traumatic for many priests. Donald B. Cozzens, in his book, *The Changing Face of the Priesthood*, has outlined the many challenges facing the priesthood today.[31] He speaks of the change from the cultic model of priesthood, where the priest was primarily seen as 'the man of the sacraments', to a model where the priest is portrayed as the *servant-leader* of the Christian community. He covers such issues as the self-identity of priests, homosexuality and the priesthood, the challenges posed by priestly celibacy, the authority crisis in the church, the intellectual crisis among priests and the tragic involvement of some priests in child sexual abuse.

We cannot afford to underestimate the betrayal of the gospel by those priests who have been involved in child sex abuse or the deep trauma suffered by their victims, which has been compounded by the slowness of church authorities in reaching out to them with compassion and love and in bringing the perpetrators to justice and, in so far as is possible, to healing. Jesus gave a dire warning: 'If any of you put a stumbling block before one of these little ones who believe in me, it would be better for you if a great millstone were fastened around your neck and you were drowned in the depth of the sea.'[32] 'Let the little children come to me, and do not stop them,' Jesus said, 'for it is to such as these that the kingdom of heaven belongs.'[33] The behaviour of priests who have been child sex abusers has not only blighted the lives of many victims but has also severely dented the morale of fellow priests world-wide, contributing as it does to a breakdown in trust between priests and people.

While all these points are valid, I believe that the priestly crisis has roots that go far deeper, being due in large measure to the failure of the church as community and the 'privatising' of sacramental practice. This has had a direct impact, if often an unconscious one, on the self-identity and self-confidence of priests. The traditional and primary role of the priest has been the 'administration' of the sacraments carried on in a parish in the midst of a society that was largely Christian. When this role was accepted as important, the priest won respect as well as material support. When his role begins to be seen by a growing number of people as irrelevant the priest is bound to suffer a crisis of identity.

The parish has been the basic unit of the church. Minimal membership of one's parish, through reception of the sacraments, has been seen as the primary way to ensure salvation, understood, in everyday language, as 'getting into heaven'. However there is much more to salvation than that. What we do on earth, in accordance with the teachings of Christ and in his Spirit, is of ultimate importance because 'eternal life', union with God, with one another and with the whole of creation, is not simply something that comes 'after' this life, but is already pre-

sent wherever human dignity, sisterly and brotherly communion and true freedom, are achieved. To quote Vatican
Council II once more: 'When we have spread on earth the
fruits of our nature and enterprise – human dignity, sisterly
and brotherly communion, and freedom – according to the
command of the Lord and in his Spirit, we will find them
once again, cleansed this time from the stain of sin, when
Christ presents to his Father an eternal and universal kingdom "of truth and life, a kingdom of holiness and grace, a
kingdom of justice, love and peace." Here on earth the
kingdom is mysteriously present; when the Lord comes it
will enter into its perfection.'[34]

Vatican II spelt out some of the challenges still facing
the church and its priests: 'The joys and hopes, the grief
and anguish of the people of our time, especially those
who are poor or afflicted, are the joys and hopes, the grief
and anguish of the followers of Christ as well. Nothing
that is genuinely human fails to find an echo in their
hearts. For theirs is a community of people united in
Christ and guided by the Holy Spirit in their pilgrimage
towards the Father's kingdom, bearers of a message for all
of humanity. This is why they cherish a feeling of solidarity
with the human race and its history.'[35]

'In every age, the church carries the responsibility of
reading the signs of the times and of interpreting them in
the light of the gospel, if it is to carry out its task. In language intelligible to every generation, it should be able to
answer the ever-recurring questions which people ask
about the meaning of this present life and of the life to
come, and how one is related to the other. We must be
aware of and understand the aspirations, the yearnings,
and the often-dramatic features of the world in which we
live.'[36]

'Far from diminishing our concern to develop this
earth, the expectation of a new earth should spur us on, for
it is here that the body of a new human family grows, fore-

shadowing in some way the age which is to come. That is why, although we must be careful to distinguish earthly progress clearly from the increase in the kingdom of Christ, such progress is of vital concern to the kingdom of God, insofar as it can contribute to the better ordering of human society.'[37]

Christians are called to be disciples, friends of and co-workers with Christ. 'I no longer call you slaves, because a slave does not know what is master is doing. I have called you friends, because I have told you everything I have heard from my Father.'[38] As friends of Christ, Christians are asked to 'bring before the ecclesial community their own problems, world problems, and questions regarding humanity's salvation, to examine them together and solve them by general discussion. According to their abilities the laity ought to cooperate in all the apostolic and missionary enterprises of their ecclesial family.'[39]

But how can they do this if ecclesial communities are such only in name? As Jean Vanier has pointed out: 'I doubt whether the leaders in society and in the churches today are sufficiently aware of the changing face of the young and a world crying out from its anguish and loneliness for a sense of belonging. Community is an urgent need not only for young people. Their cry is a prophetic sign of what is lacking in the world and in the church, not only for them but also for all. Today young people are seeking communities, not ones that are closed up and inward-looking but communities that are open to the universal, the international world: that are not limited to their own culture, that are not frightened ghettos but are open to the pain and injustices of the world. That is why so many flock to Taizé or join groups that are international.'

There are critical consequences for priests flowing from openness to the joys and anguish of our time. There are many people, with no affiliation to the church, who seek to address the grief and anguish of our world. Priests generally do not see themselves as competent in 'reading the signs of the times' in ways that address the social, political, cultural and economic problems of the day. At best they may be voices of support; at worst they can be naïve in the ways of the world. Since the good news of Christ has to address not only the strictly religious dimensions of men and women's lives but also the social, cultural, economic and political areas of life as well, the problem for the priest is that his inadequate theological training, and perhaps his personal lack of theological updating, have not always prepared him to engage with the grief and anguish of the people of our time in very effective ways.

Many of the answers that are required in addressing the anguish of our time involve bringing about change in the structures of society and *the cultural attitudes that give rise to them.* Due to their inadequate training, priests, more often than not, are left in the dark about concrete ways of interpreting the signs of the times in the light of the teaching of Christ and of the church. They limit what they say and do to what they were taught once and for all in the seminary or they simply interpret real-life happenings like any other man in the street, blurting out what they see in their own way and perhaps adding some hasty justification from the gospel that is highly questionable. Such justifications may be rejected for good reasons by some and simply judged superfluous by others. What all this implies is that the system for training priests needs to be radically overhauled so that they, together with the ordinary faithful, can bring the gospel to bear on society's problems much more realistically.

Some, who see religion as a means of maintaining the status quo in society, are keen to keep the priest 'in the sacristy'. Others want to change society, and see the priest's lifestyle and historical role as preventing him from dealing with the urgent problems of the day – another reason why priests may feel marginalised.

In the light of what we have said about the church as a community and its sacramental practice, what can we say about the role of the priest in the twenty-first century? Since all Christians are called upon not only to 'pray, pay and obey' and participate in the sacramental life of the church but also to play an active role in bringing the good news of Christ to the world, one has to ask about the specific role of the priest. Will pulpit preaching and administration 'from above' sustain and nourish the People of God? Will the priest simply continue to be a sacramentalist and a specialist of the world above?

Vatican II insists that much more is involved. Priest-leaders are called upon to form genuine communities of faith. 'The office of pastor is not confined to the care of the faithful as individuals, but is properly extended to the formation of a genuine Christian community.'[40] One has to ask how prepared priests are for the task of community building. If communities are essential so that Christians can have a real sense of belonging to the church and live out their lives together in service to humanity, priests need training in community building, in finding ways of bringing people together, sharing the Word of God with them and making the presence of the risen Christ, through creative sacramental activity, a reality for them. We have already noted what a challenge this is in contemporary culture.

Karl Rahner has described the priest as the man to whom the *Word* has been entrusted. 'The word which is entrusted to the priest as gift and mission is the *efficacious* word of *God* himself. It is the word of God. The priest is not speaking of himself. It is the word of *God*. It is spoken by God ... and brings the inner and most intimate light of God into the darkness of man. It enlightens the man who comes into the world and admits God himself into man through the faith which it awakens .... The word, whose proclamation Christ has entrusted to the priest, is an *efficacious* word ... The word first translates the love of God into man's sphere of existence *as* love, to which man can re-spond.'[41]

But God's Word of love is challenging and demanding, even frightening. 'Love one another.' 'Love your enemies.' 'Bring good news to the poor.' 'Take up your cross.' There will always be a cross somewhere in the Christian solution to evil: a cross of the pain involved in not returning blow for blow; a cross of the natural, human bitterness felt in the experiencing of hatred and returning love in its place, or receiving evil and doing good; a cross reflected in the near impossibility of counting oneself blessed in the midst of persecution, or of hungering and thirsting after justice, or in being merciful and peacemakers in a world which un-derstands neither.

Perhaps we priests are afraid to teach the gospel in all its fullness. If we challenge people too much they may fol-low the example of the young man in the gospel who went away sad because he found Jesus' challenge too much to take. Yet, Jesus loved him.[42] Are we afraid to challenge people to be 'in communion', in community, with one an-other – are we afraid to be vulnerable and be 'in commu-nion' with ourselves? Do we fear that if we preach Christ crucified, and all that that means for the millions of people 'crucified' in our world, there will be fewer people in the pews, with all the financial consequences that flow from that? Jesus too had to face that problem but he did not water down his teaching and 'many of his disciples re-turned to their former way of life and no longer accompa-nied him.'[43] Speaking the efficacious word is always risky: many have died for so doing.

The role of the priest, then, should be that of a builder of the Body of Christ, gathering men and women around him, sharing the word of God with them, and forming communities of faith, hope and love that take seriously the task of carrying on Christ's mission in the world. This is a difficult challenge especially in a world where social cohesion has broken down and where people tend to withdraw into the narrow world of personal relationships with family and close friends. In such circumstances, priests can easily become isolated and experience a lack of connectedness with the very people they are called on to serve.

Vatican II insists that priests must 'prepare themselves by careful study to enter into dialogue with the world and with people of all shades of opinion: let them have in their hearts above all these words of the council: "Since the human race today is tending more and more towards civic, economic and social unity, it is all the more necessary that priests should unite their efforts and combine their resources under the leadership of the bishops and the Supreme Pontiff and thus eliminate division and dissension in every shape and form, so that all humanity may be led into the unity of the family of God."'[44] One has to ask whether the current demands of parochial administration allow for such study, such dialogue and for the type of prayer that will sustain priests if they take the demands of Vatican II seriously.

'Pastors will not always be so expert as to have a ready answer to every problem that arises; this is not the role of the clergy: it is rather the task of lay people to shoulder their responsibilities under the guidance of divine wisdom and with careful attention to the teaching authority of the church.'[45] So one could imagine, for example, a basic community of professional people and those who are marginalised, striving to make a decisive impact on the grief and anguish of a local community in the light of divine revelation. The priest-leader should be able to *interpret the scriptures* for them and then, in the light of the gospel, the community would prayerfully call on the professional expertise of some and the practical experience of the marginalised as they speak out of their experiences and sufferings. In this way, the priest would not be working in isolation but prayerfully helping to bring the light of the gospel to bear on real-life situations.[46]

The sacraments reflect important stages of human development: birth, growing up, coping with human relationships, working, marrying and growing old and dying. Within the Christian community such moments should be made sacred, enabling them to become effective signs of the presence and grace of the living Christ. The sacraments are *means*, not ends in themselves: they help form and sustain the Christian community, enabling it to grow in the love of Christ as well as looking outwards to the service of humankind. Each sacrament is meant to signify the reality of Christ's presence among his people and the mission he entrusts to them. Hence priests have the duty to awaken people to the reality of what is taking place at each sacramental moment since each one signifies, in a particular way, both the presence of Christ to his people and his call to the community to address 'the joys and hopes, the grief and anguish of the people of our time, especially those who are poor or afflicted.' We see this exemplified most profoundly in the Eucharist, a sign drawn from the human experience of the family meal where love is shared and people are not depersonalised, each one finding his or her rightful place at the family table. In the eucharistic celebration all are brothers and sisters at the table of the Lord. The whole purpose of the 'breaking of bread' is *koinonia*, the binding of the faithful to Christ and to each other by uniting themselves to Christ's own total self-giving to the Father so that they can 'Go in peace *to love and serve the Lord.*'

As Vatican II insisted, the church is at the service of humanity. While it is easy to proclaim this, there are practical, unforeseen consequences for its *modus operandi* and especially for the work of priests. The traditional image of the priest as the 'man of the sacraments' was taken to mean that he provided a service that had direct, salvific value because it was seen to lead to the liberation of individuals from their sins. This was the aim of private confession, baptism, anonymous communion and the anointing of the sick. This same outlook determines the way many parishes still operate.

However, individual liberation from sin alone does not bring about liberation from poverty, hunger, ignorance and exploitation: such evils can only be overcome by attacking the structures of society and the cultural attitudes that give rise to them. Jesus' teaching, especially his parables, was always a call to 'conversion', to a change of mind and heart, on the part of his disciples because, in effect, he wanted them to address the underlying cultural attitudes that demeaned the poor, the suffering and the outcasts of the world. It is the duty of priests to go on calling people to such conversion, one that involves not only an individual examination of conscience but one that also focuses, communally, on the wider social context.

If priests are called upon to build up basic Christian communities through shared prayer, formative sacramental practice and the raising of the consciousness of the Christian community, *in the light of divine revelation*, to the grief and anguish of our times, what is the priest to do about those Christians who see religion simply as a private affair between oneself and God?

Karl Rahner addressed this question. 'The transformation of existing parishes into living basic communities of course presupposes that the parish priest inaugurating and leading it has the right and the courage to some extent to "neglect" baptised Christians in his parish who cannot be integrated into the new basic community, and to concentrate more on those who are ready, or can make themselves ready, to share in sustaining it. Of course a basic community should not try to be so intense and efficient as to become a closed sect with members and office-holders only interested in one another. An "integration" of this type would be wrong. But even if this danger is avoided, in view of the limited pastoral and missionary resources at the disposal of the parish priest and others involved in such change, the formation of a living basic community out of a traditional parish will not be possible except by doing without – in practice, if not in principle – a number of people belonging to the parish, if only because they will not want to fulfill the very serious demands which the new community makes on them. No attempt will be made to impose these requirements in a legal form, but the new lifestyle involved in them will in practice lead some people to dissociate themselves from the parish to a greater degree than formerly when they looked to the parish only for the satisfaction of their wholly private "religious needs".'[47]

It is important to restate that basic communities have a duty to maintain unity with the worldwide church. Observing the laws of the whole church, united with it and its bishops, they must not try to develop any sectarian or heretical theologies of their own, but remain open in a self-critical spirit, in truth and love, to the life of the whole church and its worldwide mission since no one community can address all the problems facing humanity. The priest, as servant/leader of the community, under the leadership of the bishops and the Pope, is the link between the local community and the worldwide church in its efforts to enable the coming of God's kingdom on earth.

Finally, it is important to recognise that, just as the non-ordained members of the church need to find a renewed sense of community and a sense of *belonging* within the universal church, so do priests. They need communities of men and women (not merely of fellow priests) who can support them in their work and prayer. Priests can, at times, become very isolated, content to live in clerical ghettos that isolate them from the daily ups and down of most peoples' existence, especially that of the poor. As fellow-pilgrims, and shedding all notions of personal mystery, magic and authoritarian attitudes, priests should be able to share the joys and sorrows of other peoples' lives as they deepen their own faith, hope and love. Individualism can be arrogant, whereas people 'in communion' tend to grow in realism and humility. If the crisis facing the priesthood is to be overcome and the downward spiral in priestly vocations is to be halted, priests need to be part of such communities.[48]

New seeds of hope do already exist in many areas of church life. New community groups are springing up here and there and they need the endorsement and support of the hierarchy. New forms of Christian community may well emerge from within existing parish structures, but it will not be easy to move from the traditional view of parish. However, if we don't foster the creation of basic communities, the drop in vocations will continue and leave the priest with a growing burden of work. He will continue to face a wearisome and crushing time, with little time for study, reflection and prayer. The challenges are indeed formidable but if we accept the orientations of Vatican II, we cannot continue to keep the priest in his present role without deepening his crisis of identity and contributing to the crisis of priestly vocations in the church. If the priest's role simply continues as heretofore, ageing priests, with their ageing congregations, may indeed begin to see themselves as lumbering dinosaurs.

Epilogue

In Judaism God was understood to reveal himself to the people primarily in and through their history, as well as through the Law and the prophets. The early Christians did not differ from this but believed that God had revealed himself particularly in and through the life, teaching, miracles, death and resurrection of Jesus. By the time John's gospel came to be written, the early church could affirm that 'No one has ever seen God. It is the only Son, who is close to the Father's heart, who has made him known.'[49]

As the early community, and later the wider church, reflected on who and what Jesus was, it gradually came to the conclusion that he was both true man and true God. They understood that Jesus, the man who walked this earth some two thousand years ago, was the very presence of God in their midst. John's gospel quotes Jesus as saying, 'Whoever has seen me has seen the Father. How can you say, "show us the Father"? Do you not believe that I am in the Father and the Father is in me? The words that I speak to you I do not speak on my own. The Father who dwells in me is doing his works."'[50] Those who had known him saw in Jesus such trust in God, such blazing honesty, such tenderness, such love for humanity that for them he was, as St Paul wrote in his letter to the Colossians, 'the image of the invisible God'. (1:15) As the Christmas liturgy puts it, 'In him we see our God made visible and so are caught up in the love of the God we cannot see.' Jesus' humanity mediates the presence of God because he is in full communion with God.

Jesus is the unique point of intersection between God

communicating his very Self and a human being who opened his heart and deepest self to God in the fullest way possible. God identified himself fully with humanity in Jesus. God reached deep into the life of Jesus and Jesus responded in such a loving surrender to God that it can be truly said that Jesus is 'God made man'. God, of course, is in relationship to all human beings and is present in all of creation, however obscurely, but never as intensely as God is in Jesus of Nazareth. The God-Man relationship in Jesus is absolutely unique. It is not as if God came on earth and walked around pretending to be a man: rather that God entered fully and unconditionally into human existence in the person of Jesus so that when the apostles experienced Jesus, they also experienced God as personally present in him, even if they and the church were very slow in coming to this realisation.

Jesus possessed a psychology, a culture, a genetic make-up, gender and class all his own. As Sara Maitland colourfully puts it, 'to put it bluntly, the eternal Logos, whose glory we beheld and from whom we receive grace upon grace, was potty trained – and presumably rather well potty-trained since he did not grow up seeking consolation by conquest, affirming his masculinity over the mother's ownership of his bodily production, by despising women, nor having a cringing fear of those in authority.'[51] Like all men he had to grow in wisdom. As such, his knowledge could not in itself be unlimited: it was exercised in the historical conditions of his existence in space and time. This is why the Word of God could, when he became man, 'increase in wisdom and in stature, and in favour with God and man',[52] and would have to inquire for himself about what one in the human condition can learn only from experience. This corresponded to the reality of his voluntary emptying of himself, taking 'the form of a slave'. But at the same time, this truly human knowledge of God's Son expressed the divine life of his person. The human nature of God's Son, *not by itself but by its union with the Word*, knew and showed forth in itself everything that pertains to God in his relationship with humanity. Such is first of all the case with the intimate and immediate knowledge that the Son of God made man has of his Father. The Son in his human knowledge also showed the divine penetration he had into the secret thoughts of human hearts.'[53]

It is important to realise what is at issue here. Jesus, like any other human being, had to grow up and learn from experience. He could not 'tune into his divinity' as it were and tell the apostles that men would land on the moon in the twentieth century! Rather God entered fully into human life in Jesus in such a way that a first century human being and the divine interpenetrated each other. Jesus emptied himself of divinity in order to become fully human.[54] But, as he grew and matured, he tapped into the divine depths of his being, 'incarnating' the Word of God, and making it demonstrably human. This he did through his prayer, by overcoming temptation, healing the sick, combating evil and, despite rejection, abuse and terrible suffering, continuing to trust the One he so intimately called 'Abba'. He lived his life with such blazing honesty that he enfleshed, incarnated, sacramentalised, in the most perfect way possible, God's presence among us.

Jesus had a personality and self-consciousness all his own. He was a man of his time, deeply influenced by his culture. Mary and Joseph and, no doubt, his 'brothers' James, Joseph, Judas, Simon and his sisters, his peers, the education he received in Nazareth, the people of his village, the influence of John the Baptist, all helped to form his mind and heart.

He possessed a very strong sense of intimacy with the unimaginable mystery we call God. So deep was this relationship with the one he called 'Abba' (Dear Father) that, as the Letter to the Hebrews says of him, he reflected 'the

EPILOGUE							139

brightness of God's glory and was the exact likeness of
God's own being.' Jesus, of course, does not reflect God in
his physical appearance, or in his maleness, or in his
Jewishness but rather in his creative energy and love for
humanity expressed in his message, his ministry, his love
of the poor, his suffering and, above all, in his death and
resurrection. God's Self-revelation in Jesus is an expression of his love and forgiveness as well as of final victory
over death. Jesus also reflected God's inner being by gathering around himself a small community of disciples who
were to love one another and give their lives in service to
humanity, reflecting the foundational community of all
communities, the Trinity, Father, Son and Spirit.

Jesus was a man of faith who prayed, was tempted and
could even feel abandoned by God. While the New
Testament tells us that Jesus was 'without sin', this simply
means that he was so radically centred on God that he was
able not to sin. He could make mistakes and get things
wrong like any other human being but he was always and
consistently a moral person, one with the Father, sharing
God's dream for the world.[55]

The whole focus of Jesus' message was the coming of
the reign of God and the re-gathering of the people of God
at the end-time. Jesus did not make himself the direct object of his preaching. His whole identity, personality and
mission were absorbed into and defined by the spreading
of God's kingdom. He was caught up wholly in God and
in God's dream of liberating and reconciling humanity. He
was concerned with matters of life and death and about
what is ultimately most important in life.

For many people today the belief that there is a God
with a dream for humanity is either dismissed as fanciful
or simply ignored. However everyone has a 'god', something or someone they put first, be it money, power, prestige, self, spouse, career. Whatever people put first becomes their god. But, as Jesus pointed out, 'no one can

serve two masters; for a slave will either hate the one and love the other, or be devoted to one and despise the other. You cannot serve God and wealth.'[56] Like the ordinary person in the street, priests and bishops too can put money, power, prestige, self, career or security first, failing in the process to reflect Jesus' total self-giving, his self-emptying for the sake of a broken world.

In failing to build faith-filled communities where people can share God's word and celebrate the presence of Christ in their midst, where they can rejoice together, mourn together, delight in each other and make others' conditions, especially those on the margins, their own, Christians and Christian leaders betray the gospel, and this is another reason why, for so many, God is missing but not missed.

In his own day, the crowd saw Jesus as a prophet and later, after he cast the sellers from the Temple, he was, for a time at least, hailed as a Messiah. The people of Galilee saw him as a wonder worker who had compassion on their suffering, alleviating their distress. He was a noted miracle worker. The well off saw him as a subtle narrator of parables or a vigorous debater who checkmated his opponents in controversies. To his close followers he was the man who called God 'Abba', addressing God with child-like trust, intimacy and readiness of access. He made such an impression on them that they felt he was a special 'Son of God', and later his disciples lavished him with such titles as Messiah, King, Lord of Lords. As Christians reflected on his life, death and, above all, his resurrection they came to see him indeed as true God and true man.

Today, as down the centuries, Jesus, who rose from the dead and lives among his people, asks the same question, 'Who do *you* say that I am?'[57] As John P. Meier put it, 'Jesus gives no indication of suffering an identity crisis or of a desperate need to define himself. He seems to have been quite sure of himself. Unfortunately, no one else was!'[58] As

Jesus, quoting Isaiah, reminded his disciples, 'This people will listen and listen, but not understand; they will look and look, but not see, because their minds are dull, and they have stopped their ears and have closed their eyes.'[59]

Notes

INTRODUCTION
1. Kitty Ferguson, *The Fire in the Equations. Science, Religion & The Search for God*, Bantam Books, 1995
2. Pope John Paul II, *Redemptor Hominis*
3. John Francis Kavanaugh, *Following Christ in a Consumer Society*, Orbis Books, 1983
4. Mark 4:1-20

PART ONE

Chapter 1
1. 2 Peter 3:10
2. Romans 8:22ff
3. John Polkinghorne, *One World*, SPCK 1993
4. Sara Maitland, *A Big-Enough God*, Mowbray 1995

Chapter 2
5. Hebrews 1:3
6. John 14:9
7. Matthew 25:42-44
8. Etty Hillesum, *Etty, a Diary, 1941-43*, Jonathan Cape, 1983
9. Margaret Spufford, *Celebration*, Collins, Fount Paperback, 1989
10. Isaiah 42:14
11. Romans 8:31-39
12. Philippians 2:12

Chapter 3
13. 1 Corinthians 6:14
14. Quoted in Elie Weisel, *Night*, Farrar, Straus & Giroux, 1960
15. 1 Corinthians 1: 20-28
16. Mark 9:23
17. Matthew 17:20
18. Isaiah 43:1
19. Ignatius of Loyola
20. Mark 4:26-29

Chapter 4
21. Leviticus 24:19-20
22. Exodus 20:13
23. Exodus 21:12
24. Exodus 21:15-17
25. Numbers 15:32-36

26. Vatican II, *Dogmatic Constitution on Divine Revelation*, Number 11
27. Vatican II, *Dogmatic Constitution on Divine Revelation*, Number 12
28. Matthew 5:38-39
29. Luke 6:27-31
30. Matthew 22:37-40
31. Romans 12:19-21

PART TWO

Chapter 5
1. John P. Meier's three volumes entitled *A Marginal Jew. Rethinking The Historical Jesus,* published by Doubleday
2. Mark 6:1-4
3. Prophets were not men or women who foretold the future but people intensely sensitive to the history of human suffering and to the fact that those who made the people suffer were estranged from God. The prophet, in the light of human suffering, loudly proclaimed how things had to change if human beings were to be reconciled with one another and with God. They foretold the coming of freedom, liberation from suffering and reconciliation with God in a visionary way, rather like Martin Luther King with his famous 'I have a dream' speech.
4. Matthew 3:2 and Mark 1:15
5. Matthew 15:24

Chapter 6
6. Ephesians 1: 9-10
7. Matthew 26:52
8. *Clashing Symbols. An Introduction to Faith and Culture,* Michael Paul Gallagher SJ, Paulist Press, 1997
9. John 18:36
10. John 17:22
11. Mark 10:23-27
12. Matthew 13:33
13. Mark 4:30ff
14. Galatians 1:13-16
15. Luke 17:21
16. Luke 6:20
17. Matthew 6:24
18. Mark 10:23-27
19. Luke 16:19-31
20. Raymond E. Brown, *An Introduction to the New Testament*, Doubleday, 1997
21. Matthew 5:3
22. Matthew 20:16
23. 1 Timothy 6:17-19

24. Bonnie Thurston, *Fruit of the Spirit*, The Liturgical Press, Minnesota, 2000
25. Matthew 23:1ff
26. *Jesus before Christianity*, Albert Nolan, Claretian Publications,1985
27. Mark 10:42-45
28. Matthew 23:4
29. Mark 2:23-28
30. Mark 2:15-17
31. John 4:1-42
32. 1 Corinthians 2:9
33. Ephesians 1:10
34. Matthew 6:33
35. Matthew 5:43ff
36. Mark 11:18

Chapter 7
37. 1 Corinthians 15:12-14
38. The empty tomb prompted a cover-up. When the guards at the tomb related what had happened, the priests and elders devised a plan to give them a large sum of money to say that the disciples had come by night to steal the body away while they slept. Matthew 28:11-15
39. The Pharisees were a religious-political group of devout Jews who emphasised the zealous and careful study of the Mosaic Law. They possessed a normative body of traditions, which went beyond the written Mosaic Law, and which they wished to see accepted by the whole people of Israel. The Sadducees were also a religious-political group but drawn mainly from among aristocratic laymen and members of the high-priestly families. Generally speaking, they lacked a following among the common people. They rejected some of the beliefs favoured by the Pharisees most notably the latter's belief in the resurrection of the dead.
40. Luke 24:15-16
41. Luke 24:36-37
42. See, for example, Luke 24: 13-35
43. John Polkinghorne, *One World. The Intersection of Science and Theology*, SPCK, 1993
44. Quoted in *Vision 2000. Praying Scripture in a Contemporary Way*, Mark Link SJ, Tabor Publishing, Allen, Texas, 1992
45. 1 Thessalonians 4:14
46. Matthew 25:31-46
47. Dom Helder Camara, *Hoping Against All Hope*, Claretian Publications, Quezon City, 1984
48. 1 Corinthians 15:20
49. 1 Corinthians 2:9
50. *The Church in the Modern World*, Documents of Vatican II, No. 39
51. *The Church in the Modern World*, Documents of Vatican II, No. 39

52. John 14:1-3
53. 2 Peter 3:13
54. Revelation 21:1-4

Chapter 8
55. Gerald O'Collins SJ, *The Calvary Christ*, SCM Press, 1977
56. Luke 22:42
57. Matthew 21: 33-39
58. Matthew 3:17
59. Mary Grey, *Redeeming the Dream*, SPCK, 1989
60. John 19:30
61. John 14:16,26
62. 1 Corinthians 15:45; 2 Corinthians 3:17; Philippians 1:19
63. John 3:8
64. *The Church in the Modern World*, Documents of Vatican II, No. 22
65. Edward Schillebeeckx, *God Among Us. The Gospel Proclaimed*, SCM Press, 1983
66. 2 Peter 3:10
67. 1 Corinthians 6:14
68. Edward Schillebeeckx, *God Among Us*, SCM Press, 1983
69. 1 Corinthians 2:9

Chapter 9
70. Vatican II, *Declaration On The Relation Of The Church To Non-Christian Religions*, No. 4
71. Vatican II, *Declaration On The Relation Of The Church To Non-Christian Religions*, Nos. 2 &3
72. Vatican II, *Declaration On The Relation Of The Church To Non-Christian Religions*, No. 2
73. Vatican II, ibid
74. John Carmody, *Cancer and Faith*, Twenty-Third Publications, Mystic, Connecticut, 1994
75. 1 Timothy 2:4
76. John 13:35
77. Matthew 28:11-15
78. 1 John 4:8
79. Luke 7:9
80. Luke 10:29
81. Mark 7:24-30
82. Vatican II, *Non-Christian Religions*, No. 2
83. John Paul II, *Message to the People of Asia*, Manila, 2 March 1981

Chapter 10
84. Mark 9:47-48
85. 1 John 4: 8ff
86. Mark 10:27

87. *Catechism of the Catholic Church*
88. 1 Timothy 2:4
89. 1 John 3: 14-15

Chapter 11
90. Isaiah 55:8
91. Matthew 26:39
92. Kitty Ferguson, *The Fire In The Equations*, Bantam Books, 1995
93. Joshua 10:12-14
94. Matthew 17:24-27
95. For a detailed discussion of Jesus' miracles, see John P. Meier, *A Marginal Jew. Rethinking the Historical Jesus*, Volume Two, Doubleday, 1994
96. Mark 2:1-12. See also John 5:1-9, Mark 10:46-50, Mark 8:22-26, John 9:1-7, Mark 7:31-37, Matthew 8:5-13
97. Matthew 11: 4-6
98. Luke 7:11-17
99. John Polkinghorne, *One World. The Interaction of Science and Theology*, SPCK, 1993
100. John 11:1-44
101. John P. Meier, *A Marginal Jew. Rethinking the Historical Jesus*, Volume Two, page512, Doubleday, 1994
102. Mark 9:23
103. Mark 11:23
104. See Mark 4:35-41, 5:25-34, 9:14-29, 10: 46-52, Matthew 9:27-31, 15:21-28, 17:14-21, Luke 8:22-25, 8:43-48, 18:35-42, John: 10:22-27
105. Luke17: 11-19
106. Matthew 13: 54-58
107. Mark 9:38-40
108. Revelation 21:1-4
109. Kitty Ferguson, *The Fire in the Equations*, Bantam Books, 1995

PART THREE

Chapter 12
1. Documents of Vatican II, *The Church in the Modern World*, No. 7
2. Karl Rahner, *The Shape of the Church to Come*, SPCK, London 1974
3. M. Scott Peck, *The Different Drum*, Arrow Books, 1990
4. M. Scott Peck's *The Different Drum – The Creation of True Community* spells out the dynamics for the creation of genuine communities.
5. Fundamentalist groups often have a very strong sense of community and care for their members in loving ways. Their emphasis on a strong love for Jesus has an enormous appeal and is one of the reasons why they attract so many followers. 'Roman Catholics once did quite well on that, in our popular devotions. We may have lost some of that ethos in the laudable development of liturgical language that is less emotional. Nevertheless, the love of Jesus is an enormous attraction within

Christianity. When people encounter it, and it seizes them emotionally, it sweeps them off their feet. There is no reason on earth why the love of Jesus cannot be proclaimed by the mainline churches with an equal sense of appropriateness. It was not to a fundamentalist, but to Peter, that in John 21 Jesus three times placed the demand, "Do you love me?"' Raymond E. Brown, *Responses to 101 Questions on the Bible*, Geoffrey Chapman, 1991

6. Karen Armstrong, *The Battle for God*, Ballantine Books, New York, 2000

7. Mark 10:27

8. Luke 9:23, Matthew 16:24, Mark 8:34

9. 1 Corinthians 12:12-14

10. Acts 2:42

11. John 13:35

12. See for example, St Paul's first letter to the Corinthians, 7:10,12

13. Acts 6:1-6

14. Documents of Vatican II, *The Church in the Modern World*, No. 1

15. M. Scott Peck, *The Different Drum*, Arrow Books, 1990

Chapter 13

16. Dermot A. Lane, *The Reality of Jesus*, Veritas Publications, 1975

17. John 14:16, 26

18. Matthew 18:20

19. E. Schillebeeckx OP, *Christ the Sacrament of Encounter with God*

20. 1 Corinthians 12:13, 27, 28, 26.

21. Acts 1:8

22. John Francis Kavanaugh, *Following Christ in a Consumer Society*, Orbis Books, 1983

23. Acts 2:46

24. John 13:1-17

25. Matthew 20:25-28

26. Matthew 5:23

27. Juan Luis Segundo SJ, *The Sacraments Today*, Gill and Macmillan, 1980

28. Romans 8:9

29. Vatican II, *The Church in the Modern World*, No. 38

30. Two traditional theological principles are at work here: *ex opere operato* and *ex opere operantis*. Each sacrament is efficacious, that is to say, it causes what it signifies whenever the minister performs the rite *with the intention of doing what Christ and his church intends.* So in baptism, a person is immersed in the mystery of Christ present in his community, the church. In the eucharist community members receive the body and blood of Christ (*Ex opere operato*). However, the way people approach a particular sacrament determines its fruitfulness. (*Ex opere operantis*) If, for example, a young person is confirmed simply because his class at school are being confirmed but is not raised in the practice of the faith, the sacrament may well be unfruitful in his or her life.

148   THE MISSING GOD WHO IS NOT MISSED

Chapter 14
31. Donald B. Cozzens, *The Changing Face Of The Priesthood*, The Liturgical Press, Minnesota, 2000
32. Matthew 18:6
33. Matthew 19:14
34. Documents of Vatican II, *The Church in the Modern World*, No. 39
35. Documents of Vatican II, *The Church in the Modern World*, No. 1
36. Documents of Vatican II, *The Church in the Modern World*, No. 4
37. Documents of Vatican II, *The Church in the Modern World*, No. 39
38. John 15:15
39. Documents of Vatican II, *Decree on the Apostolate of Lay People*, No. 10
40. Documents of Vatican II, *Decree on the Ministry and Life of Priests*, No. 6
41. Karl Rahner SJ, *Priest and Poet. Theological Investigations*, Volume 3
42. Mark 10:22
43. John 6:66
44. Documents of Vatican II, *The Church in the Modern World*, No. 43
45. Documents of Vatican II, *The Church in the Modern World*, No. 43
46. 'Many Catholic priests are not good expositors of the Bible. At the same time there is a real interest among the laity, and they should be tapped for this service. But they have to be informed, and that task requires people with education to supply some of the basic starting insights. If as a church we recognise this as a major problem, then we should mobilise our forces in order to supply intelligent biblical leadership among Catholics. This will prevent them from becoming fundamentalists. I do not think we have done this as a church. We are very aware of trying to meet the challenge of overliberalism or of secularism. We do not sufficiently see the danger to the right.' Raymond E. Brown, *Responses to 101 Questions on the Bible*, Geoffrey Chapman, 1991
47. Karl Rahner, *The Shape of The Church to Come*, SPCK, 1975
48. Perhaps consideration should be given to the possibility of ordaining priests proposed from within the membership of basic communities. Of course that person would have to be tested with regard to suitability by the local bishop. He would have to be trained to carry out the duties required of him, in particular that of sharing the Word of God and of building Christian community. He would have to be an effective leader and possess the qualities for leadership, particularly leadership of the Eucharistic celebration. He would be ordained and assigned to a particular community, not simply and solely as the appointed representative of the hierarchy in the sense of someone who could be moved from parish to parish. If such an approach were to be considered, church leaders would have to take cognisance of how this would impact on the priest himself who, up to now, has depended on the parish and on traditional sacramental practice to provide not only his sense of identity but his source of income as well!

Epilogue
49. John 1:18
50. John 14: 9-10
51. Sara Maitland, *A Big-Enough God*, Mowbray, 1995
52. Luke 2:52
53. *Catechism of the Catholic Church*, 472-473
54. Philippians 2:6ff
55. John 17:21
56. Matthew 6:24
57. Mark 8:29
58. John P. Meier, *Rethinking the Historical Jesus*
59. Matthew 13: 14-15